REIMAGINING AMERICA

REIMAGINING AMERICA

A Theological Critique
of the American Mythos
and Biblical Hermeneutics

by

CHARLES MABEE
III

MERCER

ISBN 0-86554-148-5

All books published by Mercer University Press are produced on
acid-free paper that exceeds the minimum standards set by the
National Historical Publications and Records Commission.

Library of Congress Cataloging in Publication Data
Mabee, Charles, 1943-
Reimagining America.

(Studies in American biblical hermeneutics ; 1)
Includes bibliographical references and index.
1. United States—Religion. 2. Bible—Criticism,
interpretation, etc.—United States. 3. United
States—Intellectual life. I. Title. II. Series.
BL2525.M32   1985   230'.044   84-27335
ISBN 0-86554-148-5 (alk. paper)

• CONTENTS •

For BARBARA

my wife and fellow scholar

• SERIES INTRODUCTION •

• Studies in American Biblical Hermeneutics •

The term "crisis" appears throughout the literature of contemporary biblical scholarship. Since the demise of commonly accepted standards of interpretation, best exhibited in the biblical theologies of Rudolf Bultmann in New Testament Studies and Gerhard von Rad in Old Testament, the entire field of biblical interpretation has exploded in myriad directions in the past decade. As a result, professors in the classroom stand in the same sort of isolation from the question of the meaning of the biblical text as does the minister before the congregation. The complexity of methodologies confronting the interpreter has caused the meaning of the text to recede from view, rather than become manifest. The result is preoccupation with method itself, and with the endless task of being "up-to-date." In turn, method dominates the lines of demarcation separating the various groups of scholars occupied with ever more specialized and complex exegetical tools. Increasingly, the results of this labor are only readily accessible to those who share the same methodological preparation and interests.

When one moves from the sphere of historical-critical scholarship to other contemporary approaches to the Bible, such as Fundamentalism and Evangelicalism, the problems multiply rather than diminish. These programs of study are developing their own complexities that rival those of historical-critical scholarship. The first requirement for purposeful participation in any such reading of the Bible is acceptance of someone's methodological presuppositions. As a result, as is the case *within* historical criticism, interpreters of the Bible in America exist in isolated and alienated clusters, rather than in a community of scholars in dialogue. This division of readership may be more detrimental to the good that religion can contribute in America than the continued existence of a church divided along denominational lines. The demanding issues of our time require an ongoing conversation by biblical interpreters who themselves operate in the broadest possible theological context.

The denomination of methodological concerns has meant that the true dialogue partner with the Bible in our time has been science and technology. This is as true of the "inerrancy" controversy within Fundamentalism as of the indeterminate final shape of the documentary hypothesis within historical criticism. In either case, the potential relevance of the Bible remains hidden. The results of the narrowly conceived research of any particular interpretive community go unnoticed by an indifferent public. It is important to understand this problem within the total spectrum of biblical interpretation in America, and not merely within a given community of readers, such as historical-critical-minded university professors, fundamentalist television preachers, or mainline Protestant ministers. The autonomous conversations carried on in each of these communities have not given the Bible a fair hearing in the marketplace of ideas that generates the inner dynamics of American cultural existence. The resulting reduction in the scope of biblical interpretation defuses the inherent universalistic claims of biblical perspectives. The present state of uncertainty in biblical interpretation that has naturally evolved in the last generation has its near parallel in the field of pure science itself (see, for example, Thomas Kuhn, *The Structure of Scientific Revolutions*). In both instances, the scholarly discussion consists primarily of refinement and enlargement of intellectual paradigms held at a given moment by a given community of interpreters rather than fresh interaction with the "text" (whether a written text or the "text of the book of nature"). In either case, the public is increasingly alienated from the intellectual life of our time, and vice versa.

• Objectives of This Series •

Mercer University Press has agreed to publish a series of monographs under the title "Studies in American Biblical Hermeneutics." The series begins with this volume, *Reimagining America*. This book will introduce the entire series and function as a programmatic illustration of it by transcending the methodological preoccupations of the contemporary scene. In this book I intend to inaugurate an explicitly public reading of the Bible by addressing it in the context of the common American cultural experience. I hope to release the Bible from the confines of the positivistic, scientific, and technical framework that restricts our dialogue in today's society, and to advocate meaningful approaches that stem from the totality of intellectual life, regardless of social or institutional context. I hope to promote interdisciplinary, interdenominational, and intercommunity (religious, artistic, political, sociological, educational, anthropological, and others) conversation with the Bible as the formative text of the American experience.

This hermeneutical approach is *not* historical in the narrow sense of studying the impact of the Bible on American culture. Such a series of studies already exists through the auspices of the Society of Biblical Literature. This series complements, rather than competes with, that important one. The difference can perhaps best be exemplified chronologically: The Bible in American Culture series is past-oriented in that it is concerned with uncovering the way that the Bible has been approached in American life and letters. In contradistinction, American Biblical Hermeneutics is present- and future-oriented, since its goal is to release biblical perspectives into the central arena of our contemporary and ongoing American intellectual life.

In order to do this, it begins by allowing the concerns and "prejudices" of contemporary thought—both "secular and sacred"—to initiate the interrogation of biblical texts. *This, in fact, represents the single methodological prerequisite for the series.* Each study within the series will be generated by a problematic aspect of American culture, rather than by a problematic concern of scholarly exegesis or theology. Of course, all of the current tools of biblical criticism must be utilized in addressing these issues, and it is quite possible that new tools might emerge in the process. In this way, American Biblical Hermeneutics is explicitly and manifestly a dialogue. It takes as axiomatic Martin Buber's simple declaration that "Truth is dialogue." This series should circumvent the current impasse in biblical studies expressly by opening the doors to the reading public and incorporating its subjective participation into the process of reading the text. This, in turn, opens doors to textual meaning and conviction.

Charles Mabee
Marshall University
September 1984

· PREFACE ·

The American character is grounded in the metaphor of universal scientific and technological experiment. Nothing else comes close to unifying the view of the world for Americans, and their place in it. Some may see God at work in the experiment, others may not. But agreement on the basic framework and ground rules is required; otherwise, one may be called "un-American." As a corollary to this great social experiment, the major cultural value to appear in America has been the principle of noninterference. Some might call it freedom, and it certainly is freedom of a particular stripe—more of a freedom *from* than a freedom *for*. The intention is not to force, or even officially encourage as a civilization, any *particular* view of the human on the society at large. The goal of the experiment is not to find the intrinsic nature of the American self, but the universal nature of humanity. The rules of the experiment were established in such a way as to allow humanity to take whatever form its intrinsic nature would dictate, free from the dictatorial power of external authorities. The walls of legal separation that shielded the various social activities of Americans from one another—whether in business, education, the military, religion, government, or the like—have been constructed with the pervasive scientific optimism that has generally accompanied the whole of American existence. In a deeply sociological sense, science, technology, and America are practically synonymous terms.

It is my intention to turn to a theological consideration of the American religious experience, set in the context of the intellectual construct of experimentation. Certainly no one doubts that Americans are a religious people. Yet the relationship between science and religion in America has been far from harmonious. Why? I propose that the definitive characteristics of the American experience of science *and* religion mask a deeper disunity. Science has a fundamentally universal orientation, dealing with the problems of space, time, and matter as they exist everywhere in the universe. The Judeo-Christian tradition, on the other hand, is grounded in a particularistic view of the world. It derives all its universal perspectives from the unique religious experience of one people among many (Israel), and one human among all humans (Jesus). For Christian thought, therefore, universality must be derived particularistically; it projects its universality upon all of experience from the particular places of revelation (Israel/Jesus). Science, however, attempts to be a manifestly pure universality; it unqualifiedly selects from nature what it requires for experimentation, rather than that which is already "chosen" by another (God). This difference in starting points is really an antagonism that ought not to be obscured, and must be faced by both theologians and scientists if a meaningful dialogue is to be achieved between the religious and scientific communities and the American self is not to be left to languish with its bifurcated soul.

The goal of this theological experiment is to make a meaningful contribution to the American understanding of the root document of our religious experience, the Bible, and to explore how that new perspective might change the face of American self-understanding. It is not a historical study of the role of the Bible in American life. Such studies continually appear in the scholarly literature, and play a crucial part in analyzing the role of "America's book." However, the task here is interpretative, rather than descriptive. I will attempt to take that pervasive voice in our culture that seeks the meaning of the universally human—and not simply the American *or* the Judeo-Christian—*as a theological category*, and direct it to certain biblical texts. Not surprisingly, most of those who have profoundly voiced such concerns and produced provocative literary works have done so outside the institutional church—with no hint of an apologetic axe to grind. American intellectuals tend not to turn their backs on a sense of the sacred, in spite of the perceived narrowness of most institutional religion. They do not, to use a time-tested phrase, "throw the baby out with the bath water." But there is no doubt that the general pessimism that has swept us all in the twentieth century has had its effect at this point as well. Post-World War II literature, for example, is less explicitly influenced by the Bible than that of previous generations. Yet the voices and concerns are there to be heard. Often the cry is faint. The figures that we have selected to engage in theological conversation do so in varying degrees of explicit interest in the Bible. Yet they are of common mind in one important sense: a major component of what I have called the American mythos of exceptionality and mission is the quest for the sacred. They believe that it is the task of all thoughtful Americans to be engaged in this quest. The literary strategies through which they attack this problem are as varied as the authors. Still, the underlying intention is the same. It is incumbent upon those of us who would labor within the church to take these voices into theological account.

I wish to include a special note of thanks to Professor Howard Slaate of the Marshall University philosophy department, who made several significant suggestions and a number of smaller technical ones while reviewing the early manuscript. In addition, I am deeply indebted to the editorial staff of Mercer University Press for their work.

Finally, I would like to acknowledge the following journals for permission to rework material I previously published in their pages: "Jefferson's Anti-clerical Bible," *Historical Magazine of the Protestant Episcopal Church* 48:4 (1979): 473-81; "Benjamin Franklin's Literary Response to Dogmatic Religion," *American Journal of Theology & Philosophy* 3:2 (1982): 60-68.

PART I

INTERPRETING THE
RELIGIOUS STRUCTURE
OF AMERICAN EXPERIENCE

To understand the American mythos requires biblical, historical, and literary scholarship. Partly because these disciplines are usually carried on by specialists who pay little or no attention to the work or conclusions of those in "other fields," approaches to this problem have led to an impasse. To surmount the obstacles to understanding erected by this intellectual atomization, I propose a self-consciously hermeneutical approach that is conceptually multidimensional and interdisciplinary. I hope to establish a framework for dialogue between the American self and the biblical tradition that already is fully present in the deepest layers of the American mythos.

IMPASSES
IN CONTEMPORARY
SCHOLARSHIP

Language is the point of departure in the quest for any mythos. As a number of interpreters of American culture have recognized, language is the enabler of self-consciousness. Three scholars—Robert Bellah, Sidney Mead, and Sacvan Bercovitch—have demonstrated particular sensitivity to this issue. They approach the subject from three distinct academic disciplines, illustrating the inclusive nature of the problem. Bellah writes from the perspective of sociology, drawing on previous analyses of Eastern religion. Mead's interpretation of American religion emerges from his distinguished career as a historian. Bercovitch is a professor of American literature; of the three, he evinces the least interest in theological matters. Bellah and Mead have made a considerable impact on contemporary theological study. Bercovitch is not as well known among students of religion, but he may yet have more to offer theologically than either Bellah or Mead.

Bellah, who is widely regarded as the creator of the famous (or infamous) "American Civil Religion" category, defended his views in the controversy that followed his seminal essay by finding refuge in the words of the American poet Wallace Stevens: "We live in the description of the place and not in the place itself." Regardless of the adequacy of the category "civil religion," Bellah claimed, its appropriation and continued use by others meant that it was now a part of the culture—like it or not. "It is now part of the description of the place in which we live; and that, at a certain level, is that."[1] If civil religion is not an accurate way of describing the American mythos, it certainly has become part of the mythos of scholarship.

The emphasis on language plays a programmatic role throughout the civil-religion literature. Bellah based much of his early work in this area on speeches of American presidents—formative "theologians" of the cultural experience. Mead also gives primacy to language. In his study of American ecclesiastical and civil institutions he writes,

> I conclude that what is commonly called the relation between church and state in the United States ought to be resolved into the theological issue between the particularistic theological notions of the sects and the cosmopolitan, universal theology of the Republic.

Throughout his later work, Mead challenges American Christian theologians to articulate a view of the faith commensurate with the realities of American cultural pluralism. He makes this point explicit in the introduction to *The Nation with the Soul of a Church*.

> My point is that there is an unresolved theological issue between "America's two religions" that contributes to the anxious misery inside our society; and my purpose has been to prod some who are theologically more hip than I am into taking it up at the point in our history where it was laid on the table and largely forgotten.

For Mead the failure of Christian theologians to speak adequately

---

[1] Robert N. Bellah, "Civil Religion in America," in William G. McLoughlin and Bellah, eds., *Religion in America* (Boston: Beacon Press, 1968); "American Civil Religion in the 1970's," *Anglican Theological Review*, Supplementary Series 1 (1973): 9. Both essays are reprinted, along with other essays contributing to the civil-religion debate, in Russell E. Richey and Donald G. Jones, eds., *American Civil Religion* (New York: Harper & Row, 1974).

of their faith in the context of the post-Enlightenment world has resulted in the increased irrelevance of the church. He reminds us of the continuing propriety of the rhetoric of persuasion in the modern world, instead of the all too frequent rhetoric of coercion.[2] Finally, Bercovitch, noting his Canadian background, records the cultural shock he experienced as he confronted the "meaning" of America.

> Mexico may have been the land of God, and Canada might be the Dominion of the North; but America was a venture in exegesis. America's meaning was implicit in its destiny, and its destiny was manifest to all who had the grace to discover its meaning.[3]

Bercovitch acknowledges that America is primarily a language event. He has undertaken a detailed study of that language, with particular attention to typological hermeneutics and the jeremiad (political sermon) genre that grew out of it. Although there is general agreement among all three of these interpreters concerning the importance of language in discovering the American self, their approaches vary considerably.

In his original statement, Bellah defined civil religion as "a collection of beliefs, symbols, and rituals with respect to sacred things and institutionalized in a collectivity."

> This religion—there seems no other word for it—while not antithetical to and indeed sharing much in common with Christianity, was neither sectarian nor in any specific sense Christian. . . . But the civil religion was not, in the minds of Franklin, Washington, Jefferson, or other leaders, with the exception of a few radicals like Tom Paine, ever felt to be a substitute for Christianity. There was

---

[2]Sidney E. Mead, *The Nation with the Soul of a Church* (New York: Harper & Row, 1975) 69, ix; *The Old Religion in the Brave New World* (Berkeley and Los Angeles: University of California Press, 1977) 36ff.

[3]Sacvan Bercovitch, "The Rites of Assent: Rhetoric, Ritual, and the Ideology of American Consensus," in Sam B. Girgus, ed., *The American Self: Myth, Ideology, and Popular Culture* (Albuquerque: University of New Mexico Press, 1981) 6; see also 5-42.

an implicit but quite clear division of function between the civil religion and Christianity.

These two religions—the civil religion and Christianity—have existed side by side in American life until the present day. They differ
theologically: the civil religion is "rather unitarian" and "on the
austere side, much more related to order, law, and right than to salvation and love." During America's formative period the symbol-
ism of the "civil religion had been Hebraic without being in any
specific sense Jewish." With this background established, reflections on the death of Lincoln and Civil War soldiers ensured that
"the theme of sacrifice was indelibly written into the civil religion."
Most important, Bellah noted, "Behind the civil religion at every
point lie Biblical archetypes: Exodus, Chosen People, Promised
Land, New Jerusalem, Sacrificial Death and Rebirth."[4] This claim
helped generate subsequent studies in this field, including Cherry's *God's New Israel* and Catherine L. Albanese's *Sons of the Fathers*.[5]

A certain air of optimism seemed to pervade Bellah's original
description of the civil religion, to the degree that a number of readers charged that he was advocating civil religion rather than simply
describing it. In a subsequent article, he sought both to clarify his
position and to bring the concept up to date. The six years that had
passed brought a marked change in tone. In an introductory definition of civil religion, Bellah added a significant qualification absent from his earlier work. He now stated explicitly that the central
tenet of civil religion was that "the nation is not an ultimate end in
itself but stands under transcendent judgment and has value only
insofar as it realizes, partially and fragmentarily at best, a 'higher
law.' " Essentially, Bellah attempted to distinguish between the
evaluative question "Should the civil religion exist?" and the epis-
temological question "Does the civil religion exist?" This entailed

---

[4]Bellah, "Civil Religion in America," 9-13, 20.

[5]Conrad Cherry, ed., *God's New Israel: Religious Interpretations of American Des-
tiny* (Englewood Cliffs NJ: Prentice-Hall, 1971); Catherine L. Albanese, *Sons of the
Fathers: The Civil Religion of the American Revolution* (Philadelphia: Temple University
Press, 1976).

an accompanying distinction—one that is not always so clear—between "the *notion* of civil religion as analytical tool" and civil religion itself as "something that exists, which, like all things human, is sometimes good and sometimes bad, but which in any case is apt to be with us for a very long time." Most of the article is devoted to his prescription for restoring the health of the civil religion that does exist, making it clear that he does not intend to avoid the evaluative question. But he also states that it is wrong to conclude that he thinks that "civil religion is always and everywhere a good thing or that the American civil religion in all its manifestations is a good thing."[6]

If any lingering doubts remained that Bellah was attempting to sacralize whatever American political order happened to exist in its institutional life, these were finally brushed aside with the publication of *The Broken Covenant*. Its language was forceful and clear: "Today the American civil religion is an empty and broken shell." "The present spiritual condition of America is not very cheering," and the "main drift of American society is to the edge of the abyss." In short, Americans are "at sea . . . in a rising storm."[7]

The category of civil religion itself received a broadly generalized meaning.

> By civil religion I refer to that religious dimension, found I think in the life of every people, through which it interprets its historical experience in the light of transcendent reality. I do not want, at this point, to argue abstractly the validity of the concept 'civil religion.' I hope to demonstrate its usefulness.[8]

At this point in the development of his thought, Bellah has chosen a utilitarian terminology, rather than a conceptual or theological one. The religious characteristics that he had earlier attached to civil religion—beliefs, symbols, rituals with respect to sacred

---

[6]Bellah, "American Civil Religion in the 1970's," 8-10; italics added.

[7]Robert N. Bellah, *The Broken Covenant: American Civil Religion in Time of Trial* (New York: Seabury Press, 1975) 142, 158.

[8]Ibid., 3.

things—have melted into the broad formulation "religious dimension." The qualifications of "transcendent judgment" and "higher law" that marked his subsequent redefinition were then subsumed into the general "light of transcendent reality." An article that followed *The Broken Covenant* a year later (during the Bicentennial) even more severely limited the notion of American civil religion, dividing it between "special civil religion" (civil religion peculiar to America) and "general civil religion" (civil religion of the kind common in America in the eighteenth century, but found elsewhere as well).[9]

This erosion of the concept of civil religion raises serious questions about its adequacy. The key to the problem may well lie in the second (apologetic) article. He outlines the conditions under which "we can perhaps still learn from the civil religious tradition": (1) that we search the whole tradition, including its heretical byways as well as its mainstream; (2) that we subject everything to the most searing criticism; and (3) that we open up our search to radically different traditions "that may supplement blind spots in even the noblest strands of our own tradition."[10] The inadequacy exhibited here can be corrected only by a self-consciously hermeneutical approach that is conceptually multidimensional. Bellah himself does not, strictly speaking, transcend the realm of American thought during his numerous discussions of civil religion. Obviously, the first condition relates only to the American tradition. And Bellah does not really provide the "searing criticism" that the second condition urges. Finally, the call in the third condition to learn from radically different traditions, a subject with which Bellah is more than comfortable, really sounds quite arbitrary and seems to imply a series of brief encounters in which one takes whatever insight one can when confronting divergent traditions.[11]

---

[9]Robert N. Bellah, "The Revolution and the Civil Religion," in Jerald C. Brauer, ed., *Religion and the American Revolution* (Philadelphia: Fortress Press, 1976) 56-57.

[10]Bellah, "Civil Religion in the 1970's," 16.

[11]Bellah, "Civil Religion in the 1970's," 19, writes that "Japanese Buddhism and American Indian religion are *two of many possible examples*" (italics added).

None of Bellah's three conditions requires that the particular identity of the American self really engage in dialogue with a meaningful partner. It sounds creative, even prophetic, to ask for "searing criticism." Yet such criticism can degenerate into a moralistic exercise, bereft of vitality and the power of persuasion, unless kept in close affinity with the realities of American identity. Similarly, a haphazard jumping from tradition to tradition can leave one at the level of "mere insight," with little motivation to change one's own tradition. It is far more meaningful to select and identify intelligently the specific traditions to be held up to the light together, so that they may "communicate" with one another, and not merely speak two different messages. The study that follows is in part a proposal to eliminate the flaws in Bellah's approach by projecting an encounter between the American self and the biblical tradition that already exists at the deepest layers of the American mythos. Rather than establishing the framework for a dialogue, the American tradition in *The Broken Covenant* is surprisingly thrown back upon itself—primarily upon such early theologians as John Witherspoon and early American presidents. Such an approach is one-dimensional and ultimately unsatisfying. It fails to achieve the "searing criticism" of American life and religion that Bellah demands.

By Bellah's own admission, Sidney Mead was his "closest predecessor."[12] By the time *The Nation with the Soul of a Church* appeared (1975), Mead acknowledged that he had been "thrust willy-nilly into the center of what they call 'The Civil Religion Debate.' " This company was not all to his liking, and it is important to understand why.

> I fear that with the ever more subtle ramification of the "civil religion" topic in the hands of academic virtuosos the relatively simple points I wish to make are in danger of being lost in the shuffle. I seem to hear "a different drummer."

This "different drummer" turns out to be the strains of theological

---

[12]Ibid., viii.

discord dividing "America's two religions"—that of "religion of the Republic" and that of the denominations. Mead reiterates this point from numerous perspectives in his 1975 work and drives it home even more powerfully in the subsequent *The Old Religion in the Brave New World*. He becomes increasingly explicit in defining the relationship between what he now calls Enlightenment religion (instead of religion of the Republic or American civil religion) and denominationalism.

> I have concluded that the two stand in a relation of mutual antagonism, and are perhaps logically mutually exclusive. That is to say that practically every species of traditional orthodoxy in Christendom is intellectually at war with the basic premises upon which the constitutional and legal structures of the Republic rest. And if this *is* the case, then every convincing defense of the one tends to undermine belief in the other.

He concludes that this antagonism has had a devastating effect on the function of religion in democratic America. In fact, it has "made theology itself a shoo-in for creeping irrelevance in the modern world."[13]

Mead's diagnosis of the "wasting sickness" of organized Christianity in America corresponds interestingly to Bellah's characterization of American civil religion as a "broken shell." Both scholars shared a common concern for the state of general religious well-being in the Republic at the time of the Bicentennial. Unfortunately, Mead's prescription is too general to be of much use for constructive purposes. We learn little about what form and substance Christian theology should take in America. He does indicate that it must emphasize the sovereignty of God and human finitude. "The one most constant strand" of the theology of the Republic "has been the assertion of the primacy of God over all human institutions."

> The obverse side of the high doctrine of God as Creator and Governor of the universe was the finite limitation of the creature, man, *in every respect*. This meant that finite man could not have absolute

---

[13]Mead, *Nation*, viii; *Old Religion*, 2, 29.

assurance of final knowledge of anything, even of the existence of God and his own salvation.[14]

Such a formulation seems to bring together the religious thought of Thomas Jefferson with the theology of John Calvin, but it remains for us to cut the pattern from this fabric.

For Mead the revolutionary period was a momentous event— one that shattered the era of "Christendom" established by Constantine and the Roman Empire and ushered in "the pre-Christendom Christian principle of sole dependence on the sword of the Spirit, the Word of God." The Revolution carried with it a rhetorical shift "from coercion to persuasion." Since the American Experiment is the "attempt to institutionalize perpetual and peaceful revolution," the operative theological categories are "persuasion" and "consent."[15] But again, Mead is only suggestive in his treatment of this aspect of his thinking, leaving the details to be worked out by theologians.

Mead's desire to maintain his separate identity apart from the civil-religion debate is perhaps easier to understand after this brief discussion. Whereas Bellah and those who employed the civil-religion category focused their study on the "religious" nature of "secular" America, Mead's point is quite different. He insists that it is the responsibility of the Christian churches to catch up in their thinking with the theology of the Republic that already exists in the formative civil documents of the land. He refuses to subsume under the overarching category of "civil religion" the tension between "America's two religions." Of course, it is important to understand that Mead's perspective in the theological split is not a neutral one; he is a firm advocate of the religion of the Republic. Furthermore, as a sort of theologian of the Republic, he does not attempt a genuine dialogue with theologians of denominational

---

[14]Mead, *Nation*, 67; *Old Religion*, 84-85; see also *Nation*, 10, where he notes, "In the Republic 'the people' is the emperor. Churches exist in the Republic to remind this sovereign ruler, 'You, too, are mortal; you are not God.' "

[15]Mead, *Old Religion*, 39-40, 37; see also *The Lively Experiment: The Shaping of Christianity in America* (New York: Harper & Row, 1976) ch. 2.

Christianity. Instead, he presents the theology of the Republic more or less as a closed position.

To restore health to American Christianity requires a dialectical relationship between the received Christian tradition and the dynamic of the American self. Mead's advocacy of Enlightenment religion not only appears philosophically naive, but might also prove in the long run to be more oppressive than sectarian theology. He sees it primarily as a universal religion, transcending the provincialities of denominational particularism. He calls it "the only religion that can unify the one world created by modern technology, which is potentially the Republic of mankind."[16] Hermeneutical dialogue does not allow us to shift so quickly to universals. There are probably at least as many dangers and hindrances to truth in the guise of "universals" as in explicitly sectarian thought. It would be much more fruitful to identify a creative way to utilize the perspectives of the self *and* the religious tradition from which it springs in the least dogmatic way possible. Only then will we find the persuasive rhetoric that Mead desires.

Whereas Bellah calls us back to the moral principles of the covenantal tradition in its early Puritan and presidential forms and Mead prescribes the universal religion of the Republic, Sacvan Bercovitch offers a more radical cure for the problems that beset the religious dimension of the "American Experiment." Coming to the issue from the perspective of American literature, he has perhaps penetrated more deeply to the American self's core of meaning than any other contemporary scholar. In contrast to the jeremiads of American-born Bellah and Mead, Canadian-born Bercovitch argues for nothing less than the demythologization of the American mythos. In his view the persistence of this mythos throughout the course of American history accounts for much of the culture's woes.

> History has been making it clear for some time that the hazards of living out the dream outweigh the advantages. . . . Who knows, the errand may come to rest, where it always belonged, in the realm

---

[16]Mead, *Nation*, 9.

of the imagination; and the United States recognized for what it is, not a beacon of mankind, as Winthrop proclaimed in his *Arbella* address of 1630, not the political Messiah, as the young Melville hymned in *White-Jacket*—not even a covenanted people robbed by un-American predators of their sacred trust—but simply *goy b'goyim*, just one more profane nation in the wilderness of this world.[17]

The significance of this statement stems partly from its culminating position at the end of a decade and a half of scholarly research and writing about the American mythos and its rhetoric. As Bercovitch conceives of the nature of the mythos, it was the design of the early American Puritans "to impose a sacred telos upon secular event[s]." In terms of language, they "discovered America in scripture," proceeding "from the thing to the things signified—from Noah to Abraham to Moses to Nehemiah to 'Americanus.' Along the way, they changed the focus of traditional hermeneutics, from biblical to secular history." The exegetical tool they used to effect this transformation was typology (figuralism), which as Bercovitch and others have shown, must play a central role in the imagination of American self-understanding.

Figuralism affirms the oneness of *allegoria* and *littera-historia*, as well as the interchangeability of private, corporate, historical, and prophetic meaning (e.g., "Israel" as the believer, the entire community of the elect, the latter-day church, and the saints in New Jerusalem). The Puritans used this approach consistently, comprehensively, as a means of transforming secular into sacred identity. Thus they personified the New World as American microchrista. Thus also they combined the genres of political and spiritual exhortation, and equated public with personal welfare. In effect, they invented a colony in the image of a saint.[18]

---

[17]Bercovitch, "Rites," 35.

[18]Bercovitch, *The Puritan Origins of the American Self* (New Haven: Yale University Press, 1975) 52, 112, 114. See also Mason I. Lowance, Jr., *The Language of Canaan: Metaphor and Symbol in New England from the Puritans to the Transcendentalists* (Cambridge: Harvard University Press, 1980).

This hermeneutical approach created an "unprecedented genre of hagiography." Its rhetorical form was "America's first distinctive literary genre," the jeremiad. Bercovitch defines this genre as the "political sermon," a kind of "state-of-the-covenant address, tendered at every public occasion" such as "days of fasting and prayer, humiliation and thanksgiving, at covenant-renewal and artillery-company ceremonies, and most elaborately and solemnly, at election-day gatherings." In his later works, Bercovitch is concerned to take this genre, remove it from its original setting in life, and trace it through the course of American letters. The import of such an approach is the documentation of the way Puritan rhetoric and mythic categories were generalized into the American mythos. "The Puritan jeremiad set out the sacred history of the New World; the eighteenth-century jeremiad established the typology of America's mission."[19]

By establishing the secular foundations of the whole mythic tradition in its Puritan origins, the true self-serving nature of the mythos becomes manifest. This allows for the possibility of demythologizing, or distancing oneself from the way that Americans view the world. The positive result of this will be a lessening of the grip of nationalism that continues to plague the culture in our time. Yet as matters now stand, he notes,

> Only in the United States has nationalism carried with it the Christian meaning of the sacred. Only America, of all national designations, has assumed the combined force of eschatology and chauvinism. Many other societies have defended the status quo by reference to religious values; many forms of nationalism have laid claim to a world-redeeming promise; many Christian sects have sought, in secret or open heresy, to find the sacred in the profane, and many European defenders of middle-class democracy have tried to link order and progress. But only the American Way, of all modern ideologies, has managed to circumvent the paradoxes inherent in these approaches. Of all symbols of identity, only *America* has united nationality and universality, civic and spiritual self-

---

[19]Bercovitch, *Origins*, 115; *The American Jeremiad* (Madison: University of Wisconsin Press, 1978) 6, 4, 93.

hood, and secular and redemptive history, the country's past and paradise to be, in a single synthetic ideal.[20]

Seen in this light, the mythos of America is basically another of the oppressive ideologies of the twentieth century, even though its roots can be traced to the seventeenth. Implied is the failure of American Christians to stand up against this secular use of their traditions. Although the emphasis and perspective are different, it is as negative a reading of the state of Christianity in America as that proposed by Bellah or Mead. Again, Christian theology has not faced the particular issues of this specific horizon. It is closer to irrelevance rather than a means of salvation.

Bercovitch's analysis is sound and his message is useful, as far as it goes. But it is one thing to desacralize a mythos; it is quite another to *utilize* it in hermeneutical dialogue. Ultimately, the real point is not the truth or falsity of North American mythos, but whether or not one *accepts it as a vital component within the interpretive process*. Acceptance in this sense does not mean that the mythos is uncritically accepted as an accurate portrayal of what exists, but that one takes it as an *interpretive key* that initiates the dialogical exchange. This way of addressing the mythos is entirely absent from Bercovitch's work. Ultimately, Bercovitch never escapes the one-dimensional plane that often characterizes the descriptive historian. While he does achieve a critical dimension over and above tradition (the tradition as falsely conceived and established), he does so only on the basis of the tradition itself. It is not so much that something is inherently wrong with this approach, but that it represents a missed opportunity. To so quickly condemn a world view is to deflate it beyond recognizable benefit. Furthermore, if the mythos is as central to the self-identity of the American psyche as Bercovitch claims—and I fully agree that it is—what will be the state of the psyche when the mythos is removed? One might imagine that such crippling experience is necessary for facing up to reality, but it is far more likely an insurmountable obstacle that will appeal only to an intellectual elite with the patience to wade through the details of

---

[20]Bercovitch, *Jeremiad*, 176.

Charles Mabee

scholarly documentation supporting Bercovitch's case. At that point, one is undoubtedly preaching only to the converted anyway.

Still, Bercovitch's thorough analysis of the grammar of the American mythos, namely typological or figural thinking (especially as it was formulated by Puritan thinkers and subsequent literary figures of the American Renaissance), can serve as a basis for illustrating additional ways in which typology achieved textuality in the infant Republic. The efforts of these founders of the Republic, in turn, formed the intellectual matrix for the work of subsequent interpreters of the American mythos, such as Herman Melville and Robert Pirsig.

BIBLICAL HERMENEUTICS
AS A WAY OF ACCESS

Even if it were considered to be a desirable goal, few people today would maintain that a fully objective exegesis of the Bible (or any piece of literature) is possible. Generations of critical biblical scholars have constructed elaborate safeguards against subjective interpretation. The problem of "reading into" (eisegesis) a text the meaning that one wants to find is certainly real enough, as the history of Christian theology readily demonstrates. Fortunately, we are intellectual heirs to a host of exegetical methods that have made great progress in allowing the biblical text to speak its own message in the context of its own place and time. G. W. H. Lampe articulated the overall goal of biblical criticism, saying that it "sought to recover the true and original meaning of the literal sense, and to set the various documents comprising the Bible in their proper context in history."[1]

---

[1]G. W. H. Lampe and K. J. Woollcombe, *Essays in Typology* (Naperville IL: Allenson, 1957) 15.

Indeed, the growth of the study of the Bible outside the ecclesiastical environment after the Enlightenment, and its general alli-
ance with scientific method, escalated the value of objective
interpretation. Genuine recognition of the foreignness of the historically bound Scriptures inevitably emerged due to this conscious
distancing of the text from the world of the interpreter. Yet this extraordinary achievement has itself become increasingly problematic in recent generations, and not merely in the well-known sense
in which Rudolf Bultmann distinguished the "mythical world of the
Bible" from that of modern science and technology.[2] Any thorough
discussion of "scientific" criticism today must take fully into account the evolving way in which science itself is conceived.

Recent attacks on the supposed objectivity of science have obvious implications for all kinds of interpretive theory. Thomas S.
Kuhn initiated much of the current discussion in his ground-break-
ing book, *The Structure of Scientific Revolutions*.[3] Kuhn argued persuasively that usual scientific work stands not in primary
relationship to objective phenomena, but to the prevailing intellectual paradigms by which fields of research structure knowledge.[4]
Scientific knowledge is bound to such paradigms, and the touch-
stones of intellectual history exist at those revolutionary points
when new paradigms supplant the old by more adequately ac-

---

[2]Bultmann insisted that "the world-view of the New Testament is the language
of mythology, and the origin of the various themes can be easily traced in the contemporary mythology of Jewish Apocalyptic and in the redemption mythos of
Gnosticism. To this extent *the kerygma is incredible to modern man, for he is convinced
that the mythical view of the world is obsolete.* We are therefore bound to ask whether,
when we preach the Gospel to-day, we expect our converts to accept not only the
Gospel message, but also the mythical view of the world in which it is set. If not,
does the New Testament embody a truth which is quite independent of its mythical
setting? If it does, theology must undertake the task of stripping the Kerygma
from its mythical framework, of 'demythologizing' it." See Hans Werner Bartsch,
ed., *Kerygma and Myth: A Theological Debate* (New York: Harper & Row, 1961) 3; italics in original.

[3]Cf. Thomas S. Kuhn, *The Structure of Scientific Revolutions*, 2d ed. (Chicago:
University of Chicago Press, 1970).

[4]See ibid., 10-11.

counting for the consequences of new data. But it is a mistake, Kuhn maintained, to believe that the successive changes in paradigms evident in intellectual history lead us closer and closer to the truth.

> We are all deeply accustomed to seeing science as the one enterprise that draws constantly nearer to some goal set by nature in advance. But need there be any such goal? Can we not account for both science's existence and its success in terms of evolution from the community's state of knowledge at any given time? . . . If we can learn to substitute evolution-from-what-we-do-know for evolution-toward-what-we-wish-to-know, a number of vexing problems may vanish in the process.[5]

Kuhn saw development within the various disciplines of science, but eliminated objective knowledge of truth as a possibility. His perspective has generated much discussion both inside and outside the fields of "hard" science, and he has over time modified and refined some aspects of his position. Nevertheless the basic features of his argument have gained widespread acceptance despite the natural, built-in resistance of the scientific establishment. The impact of Kuhn's work on the nature of scientific research, and on those working in other fields,[6] has raised questions about the role of the interpreter in biblical exegesis that delve beyond the hermeneutical concerns of the Bultmann school of New Testament interpretation[7] because they *penetrate to the primary level of exegesis itself.*

It is not simply, as Bultmann argued, that historical criticism has opened up a foreign world to us, one that we must bridge hermeneutically with primary existential categories. We have not, during

---

[5]Ibid., 171.

[6]For references to Kuhn's influence on such fields as philosophy, psychology, and sociology, see Eugene Lashchyk, "Scientific Revolutions" (Ph.D. dissertation, University of Pennsylvania, 1969).

[7]See James M. Robinson and John B. Cobb, eds., *The New Hermeneutic* (New York: Harper & Row, 1964).

the past several hundred years, been neutral observers of the formative period of our religious heritage. The subjective component of exegesis has been part of our work just as surely as in earlier periods of ecclesiastical dogmatism. Only now the name of this component is science itself. Science has been the unreflected-upon part of the interpretive self in biblical exegesis during the past several centuries. Further, its achievements have been just as monumental in the literary fields as in the sciences themselves. What has emerged, however, is not the "original Bible" (the true Bible), but rather a scientifically delimited one. In short, the recovery of the "true and original meaning of the literal sense" (Lampe) of the Bible is a linguistic fiction that is fully subjective in origin. My own work begins with this necessary failure of historical criticism to eradicate the subjective component of biblical criticism. It does this by self-consciously embracing the subject and integrating it more fully into the exegetical process.

A broadly based understanding of literature eliminates the hostile way most biblical scholars treat subjectivity in interpretation. This is because literary texts generally intend to provoke the reader into completing their own meaning. Great works of art do not offer the beholder a finished product. To demand such a thing in biblical exegesis represents the turning of science into Scientism. Objectivity in this isolated sense is not true objectivity because it tends to make of the text/object something that the text is not. This false objectivity is only the manifestation of the subjective views of traditional science. We actually remain more in the domain of textual intentionality when we self-consciously relate our own necessarily subjective prejudices[8] to the interpretive act. Clearly, this subjective intentionality of all texts (simply because they are texts) exists in greater or lesser magnitude depending on their specific character-

---

[8]For an excellent discussion of the place of "prejudice" in interpretation, see Hans-Georg Gadamer, *Wahrheit und Methode*, 2d ed. (Tübingen: J. C. B. Mohr [Paul Siebeck], 1960) 261ff. Similarly, Walter L. Brenneman and Stanley O. Yarian write: "It is this combination of a self-reflective attitude integrated with a concern for object-in-situation that distinguishes the hermeneutical phenomenologists of religion from the morphological"; in *The Seeing Eye: Hermeneutical Phenomenology in the Study of Religion* (University Park: Pennsylvania State University Press, 1982) 18.

REIMAGINING   AMERICA   • 23 •

istics (especially generic ones). Some texts are meant more to inspire us to create our own literary experiences than others, but surely all texts do this to one degree or another. Ruling this component out of the exegetical process severely circumscribes the rich spectrum of meaning that characterizes all linguistic expression. As I. A. Richards succinctly observed several decades ago, "A book is a machine to think with."[9] This appreciation of the subjective component of interpretation is deeper in literary circles not burdened by the peculiar history of ecclesiastical dogma from which historical criticism has helped us to escape, only to fall victim to more complex forms of dogmatism. A more recent exponent of this insight is Wolfgang Iser, who writes that

> during the process of reading there is an active interweaving of anticipation and retrospection, which on a second reading may turn into a kind of advance retrospection. The impressions that arise as a result of this process will vary from individual to individual, but only within the limits imposed by the written as opposed to the unwritten text. In the same way, two people gazing at the night sky may both be looking at the same collection of stars, but one will see the image of a plough, and the other will make out a dipper. The "stars" in a literary text are fixed; the lines that join them are variable.[10]

The fixing of the "lines" of interpretation is not only subjective, it is also meant to be, in Iser's literary criticism. If the astronomical metaphor holds even approximately, then it is senseless to speak of a particular interpretation as being "out there" (in the text). Each reading of the text ultimately finds its own interpretation. Iser concludes that

> the reading process always involves viewing the text through a perspective that is continually on the move, linking up the different phases, and so constructing what we have called the virtual dimen-

---

[9]Quoted in Wolfgang Iser, *The Implied Reader: Patterns of Communication in Prose Fiction from Bunyan to Beckett* (Baltimore: Johns Hopkins University Press, 1974) 45.

[10]Ibid., 282.

sion. This dimension, of course, varies all the time we are reading.[11]

Iser maintains that the chronological or historical character of the interpretive act is just as much a part of the reader of the text as of the writer. In this sense, historical criticism that has helped uncover the historical quality of the biblical text needs to be taken to the next logical step to include the historical nature of the reader. It is not enough to leave such matters to theology. To proceed on the basis that there is a message in the text that the believing community is bound to interpret to the contemporary world illustrates a fundamental misunderstanding of the way a text conveys meaning. It is far more accurate to say that we are part of the meaning of the text *from the beginning*. This is the point of departure for my own hermeneutical exegesis.

A particular exegetical program has been introduced into the scholarly discussion in recent years that impinges on the question of the subject in interpretation. This is the so-called canonical criticism of Brevard Childs.[12] Childs has proposed that we treat the Old Testament as the sacred scripture of the believing community at the most fundamental level of interpretation. This is to be done not at the expense of the historical and literary insights of the various critical methods, but in recognizing their limitations. Rather than conceiving of the theologically grounded canonical status of the Old Testament as an unscientific faith environment from which the text must be extricated in order to be critically examined, he sees this "canonicity" as the key to exegesis. The emphasis in his approach is quite naturally on the text in its final (canonical) form. Frequently, for example, the redactors responsible for the final form of an Old Testament book in the history of its (oral and) written transmission provide the reader with the central meaning of a text.[13] In other instances, these redactors simply confirm the mean-

---

[11]Ibid., 280.

[12]See Brevard S. Childs, *Introduction to the Old Testament as Scripture* (Philadelphia: Fortress Press, 1979).

[13]Ibid., 71, 75ff.

ing already explicit in the received text.[14] In either case, however, the perspective within which a text became canonical determines, for Childs, all subsequent exegetical thought. It is clear that this method is grounded in the historical-critical methodologies of tradition history and redaction criticism, but it differs in that the canonical status of the final text is taken as authoritative. Older methods were typically oriented toward atomization in the way that they variously peeled back the historical layers of a text to its point of origin. Childs strives toward a holistic reintegration of the various levels of textual meaning under the rhetoric of canon, pointing out the inadequacy of atomization. More important, there is a sense in which Childs brings the question of the interpretive subject back into the mainstream of biblical exegesis. The question is whether or not he goes far enough in this direction.

The subjective element comes into play for Childs at the point where the framers of the Old Testament canon were guided by their contemporary concerns in the utilization of traditional texts. We know that these redactors were capable of giving texts whole new meanings; Childs wants to focus our exegesis precisely on this point.

> By insisting on viewing the exegetical task as constructive as well as descriptive, the interpreter is forced to confront the authoritative text of scripture in a continuing theological reflection. By placing the canonical text within the context of the community of faith and practice a variety of different exegetical models are freed to engage the text, such as the liturgical or the dramatic.[15]

In this way, Childs aims at a method that "forces" theological reflection by setting the biblical text in the tradition of interpretation of the faith community. This is obviously a step forward in allowing the subjective perspective of subsequent interpreters of a text to have a dominant say in the exegetical task. Yet it is clear that Childs

---

[14]See, for example, the way that Childs handles the book of Joshua; Childs, 247ff.

[15]Ibid., 83.

does not go as far in this direction as the work of Iser and others encourages. In significant ways, Childs does not sufficiently free himself from the methodological chaos that he hopes to escape.[16]

The problem of method remains uppermost in the approach of Childs to his exegetical work. The perspective of canon is methodologically necessary in all instances of textual interpretation. In this way, even though he takes the subjective theological perspectives of the believing community as most important exegetically, Childs continues to treat the text as object in the same basic fashion as the historical-critical method. From our contemporary standpoint, the canonical perspectives are just as objectified into the text as are the earlier layers of tradition. Childs still labors under the conception of a textual meaning "out there" by objectifying the subjective process of canonization. One still must judge his approach on the basis of method and, as a result, basic questions remain. Is the decision to allow the canonical meaning of a text to dominate other ways of gaining access to it convincing? Is the canonical interpretation inevitably more insightful than that offered by more traditional methods, especially tradition history and redaction criticism? Does the method not represent a retreat from the hard-won gains of historical criticism that made the Bible a book accessible to more general interpreters of Western experience? Does it not carry implications of a secular/sacred distinction in the modern world that is alien to the biblical texts themselves? Other readers may well raise other questions. The point is that the growing dissatisfaction with the inability of the historical-critical methods to encourage a theological encounter with the Bible should not force a retreat from viewing the Bible as a book of the world, and not simply the religious communities. To redefine the Bible as fundamentally a religious book and not a work grounded in the historical contingencies of human existence is to move away from the intention of the Bible itself. It is especially important today to resist any approach that dilutes any aspect of this holistic viewpoint. What is

---

[16]"The biblical field has grown weary of hastily-constructed theories which advocate change of direction, and which in most cases have done more harm than good"; ibid., 16.

needed today, theologically, is a way of reading the Bible that maintains the objective historical otherness of the period of its composition, yet integrates at the most fundamental level of interpretation the subjective historical concerns of the reader. Childs only produces a Bible for the church. It is my intention to broaden the dialogue with the Bible in such a way that the fullness and diversity of the American religious experience helps us to read these old texts in a new way. In order to revitalize our theology, we need to find in them that which is not only important, but important *for us*. As historically conditioned members of our culture, we really can do nothing else and remain true to our own identity.

Up to this point, I have discussed the need for reestablishing the interpretive self in the exegesis of biblical texts. The question remains, how are we to proceed? Unlike the historical critics, and even Childs himself, my task is not primarily methodological. I do not want to establish yet another method of biblical exegesis, but rather I want to contribute to the further uncovering of the interpretive self that always accompanies exegesis, whether consciously or unconsciously, and influences it deeply—often in an unconscious way. Yet the problem of method cannot be postponed indefinitely. In the search for the fundamental influences that shape the way we read the Bible in our culture, a particular field of meaning has emerged that has the power to open new vistas of theological understanding. I am referring to that cultural expression that one finds embodied in the primal mythos of exceptionality and mission. This pattern of belief is found in a wide spectrum of American literary texts, and is widely acknowledged by the scholarly community. Leaving aside the European mythos of the New World that preceded American exploration and settlement, the basic concept already exists in John Winthrop's sermon, "A Modell of Christian Charity," preached en route to North America aboard the *Arbella* in 1630. Winthrop concluded that

> we must consider that we shall be as a City upon a Hill, the eyes of all people are upon us; so that if we shall deal falsely with our God in this work we have undertaken, and so cause him to withdraw his

present help from us, we shall be made a story and a byword through the world.[17]

This concept of a "City upon a Hill" spawned centuries of exegetical study on the religious meaning of America that has persisted to our own day. From the beginning the experience of American culture has been fundamentally religious. All of us shaped by this culture are linked to this rhetoric of exceptionality and mission in a primal way. It undergirds everything that we do as a people, including the formation of our theological traditions. Many sensitive interpreters of the story of American religion have made this clear. What remains is to discover the theological meaning of this phenomenon. This can best be accomplished by taking the mythos actively into the heart of the theological task and investigating its relationship to the interpretation of Scripture.

The paradigmatic study of typological exegesis was Erich Auerbach's essay "Figura." In general, Auerbach distinguishes the modern view of history from the typological one.

> In the modern view, the provisional event is treated as a step in an unbroken horizontal process; in the figural system the interpretation is always sought from above; events are considered not in their unbroken relation to one another, but torn apart, individually, each in relation to something other that is promised and not yet present. Whereas in the modern view the event is always self-sufficient and secure, while the interpretation is fundamentally incomplete, in the figural interpretation the fact is subordinated to an interpretation which is fully secured to begin with: the event is enacted according to an ideal model which is a prototype situated in the future and thus far only promised.

This relationship between the original event and the interpretation of it (type-antitype) is grounded in the process of understanding one worldly event through another.

---

[17]Often reprinted; see, for example, Jane L. Scheiber and Robert C. Elliott, eds., *In Search of the American Dream* (New York: New American Library, 1974) 47.

The first signifies the second, the second fulfills the first. Both remain historical events; yet both, looked at in this way, have something provisional and incomplete about them; they point to something in the future, something still to come, which will be the actual, real, and definitive event.

These considerations help Auerbach make fundamental distinctions between allegory, typology, myth, and symbol. While typological interpretation is "allegorical" in the broadest sense of the term, it differs in the necessary reference to a "definite event in its full historicity." In contrast,

> Most of the allegories we find in literature or art represent a virtue (e.g., wisdom), or a passion (jealousy), an institution (justice), or at most a very general synthesis of historical phenomena (peace, the fatherland)—never a definite event in its full historicity.

Symbols and myths, on the other hand, differ from allegories by providing "a direct interpretation of life and originally no doubt for the most part, of nature." The way in which typological interpretation alone is tied to history results in the fact that "it is by nature a textual interpretation."[18]

The importance of this insight for properly addressing the mythos of America, and the particular biblical hermeneutics undergirding it, is profound. In discussing Puritan typological interpretation in New England, Perry Miller notes, "Types were not allegories or emblems or fictitious narratives, the spirit of which might be that of Christ, but they were preliminary, factual prefigurations of what Christ finally did."[19] In New England, the sacral structure of the American mythos was made possible through the use of typological exegesis of the Bible. Only in hermeneutical dialogue with the sacred may that mythos be laid bare and utilized in the process of understanding.

---

[18]Cf. Erich Auerbach, "Figura," in *Scenes from the Drama of European Literature* (New York: Meridian, 1959) 11-76, esp. 54-59.

[19]Perry Miller, *Images or Shadows of Divine Things* (New Haven: Yale University Press, 1948) 6.

One important way to accomplish this work is to investigate the role of the mythology *within* the ecclesiastical structure. Bercovitch's *The Puritan Origins of the American Self* stands as a paradigmatic study in this regard. After all, the concept *is* fundamentally an ecclesiastical one. Mason I. Lowance, Jr. has put the matter succinctly, when he observes that

> the language of Canaan—from the sermons of John Cotton to the prophetic symbols of *Walden*—is based on structural and metaphorical principles articulated by the writers of the Bible, whose guiding vision of eternal purpose pervaded every image and type and gave eschatological meaning to each historical episode. It is, then, a biblical impulse that defines America's purpose.[20]

Lowance correctly sets this "language of Canaan" in the context of the typological interpretation of Scripture. Puritan typological exegesis was grounded in a particular view of history. It pointed to persons and events in history and envisoned them as prefiguring later historical manifestations. Yet, as Conrad Cherry in *God's New Israel: Religious Interpretations of American Destiny* makes clear, the mythos that this form of exegesis engendered moved easily from the ecclesiastical sphere to that of the general culture.

> Beheld from the angle of governing myths and symbols, the history of the American civil religion is a history of the conviction that the American people are God's New Israel, his newly chosen people. . . . [this conviction] is a myth in the sense that it provides a religious outlook on history and its purpose, and by finding a place in the feelings and choices as well as in the ideas of the people, it can move them to action. . . . America has been regarded either as a "light to the nations" which by force of example will positively influence other peoples and perhaps draw them to an American haven of freedom, or as a chosen people with an obligation actively

---

[20]Mason I. Lowance, Jr., *The Language of Canaan: Metaphor and Symbol in New England from the Puritans to the Transcendentalists* (Cambridge: Harvard University Press, 1980) 4.

to win others to American principles and to safeguard those principles around the world.[21]

Here, Cherry correctly points to the same material content of the mythos for the culture at large as in its original theological formulation: (1) Exceptionality (or chosenness) and (2) mission. Several years later, Robert Jewett developed the mission component of the mythos, which he sees as especially virile since the Civil War, in a book entitled *The Captain America Complex*. At the outset of this work Jewett observes,

> A sense of mission "was present from the beginning of American history, and is present, clearly, today" as Frederick Merk put it. In its more expansive form this sense of calling was a calling to nothing short of redeeming the entire world. Albert J. Beveridge, historian and senator, claimed precisely this at the beginning of the century. "God . . . has marked the American people to finally lead in the redemption of the world. This is the divine mission of America. . . . We are the trustees of the world's progress, guardians of its righteous peace."[22]

Jewett traces this redemptive mission to Old Testament roots, attempting to temper what he calls "Zealous Nationalism" with "Prophetic Realism." I believe that a more fruitful theological method is to utilize the fabric of the mythos as an interpretive means of examining the inner depths of the Bible's meaning *for us*. If we listen to the fullness of the New World mythos, *before* we attempt to eradicate it as jingoistic ideology, it can uncover new levels of sacred dimensionality within the Bible. This is because the Bible is not simply "there" as an object to be interpreted, but exists as a literary partner waiting to engage us in theological dialogue. Be-

---

[21]Conrad Cherry, *God's New Israel: Religious Interpretations of American Destiny* (Englewood Cliffs NJ: Prentice-Hall, 1971) 21-22.

[22]Robert Jewett, *The Captain America Complex: The Dilemma of Zealous Nationalism* (Philadelphia: Westminster, 1973) 9.

cause this position is a foreign one for the ecclesiastical Bible (which stands against the world), it is necessary to begin our dialogue within the American cultural matrix of the "churchless Jesus."

·PART II·

THE
CHURCHLESS JESUS
IN FORMATIVE
AMERICAN DISCOURSE

A s founding American figures, Thomas Jefferson and Benjamin Franklin helped to establish an alternative version of the New World mythos. In doing so, they maintained the same mythic structure of exceptionality and mission that informed Puritan typology. Both saw in the American experience the establishment of a people set aside from the world for the purpose of cleansing and renewing it. However, they believed that this liberation of the human spirit would not be led by the church, but by those freed from its dogmatic grip. They represented, in short, a churchless, declericalized version of typological thinking that saw a different ''city upon a hill''—one that proclaimed release to the captives of the church as well as of the state.

Looking back, one may easily conclude that both of these men were simply participating in the general world view of the Enlightenment. One can point to the Cartesian way that they sought to escape the reach of ecclesiastical power in order to make room for the free play of individual reason. Jefferson believed that he could read the Bible himself in a more correct way than the ecclesiastical theologians, picking and choosing from contemporary biblical scholarship what best suited the particular purposes of a mind without theological training. Franklin's persona in his *Autobiography* and his captivating "Poor Richard" each represented individualists freed from both academic and theological speculation. But to stop at this point is to miss the deep connection that these men had to the New World mythos. The power of the belief that the American experience represented a new opportunity for *all* people unmistakably informs their literary endeavors. God was not afraid of truth, even though theologians might be. It was America's sacred destiny to lead the world in the unencumbered pursuit of truth, whether it be *with* the church or *in spite of* the church.

The American mythos gave such figures as Jefferson and Franklin the intellectual justification for speaking as theologians, albeit nonecclesiastical ones. Far from being disadvantageous for addressing religious matters, their roots in the mythos gave them a theological advantage over their counterparts among the clergy. While the church busied itself with trying to breathe new life into the worn-out doctrines of the old European religious traditions, men such as Jefferson and Franklin would ground their religious thought in the very freshness of the New World itself, bringing the conviction of simple clarity to underlying theological questions. They were new Adams living in a new Eden, and they had a new way of looking at the world. The mythic field of meaning that rippled from its origins in New England brought a measure of self-confidence and aggressiveness against the traditions of the past that would have made Descartes cower and disagree. The ecclesiastical hold on society had a measure of openness in both Virginia and Pennsylvania that was lacking in New England. Thus both Jefferson and Franklin approached the Bible with the new light of liberated reason. They saw it as a book of great moral resource, but one devoid of the "artificial" underpinnings of ecclesiastical authority.

But the battle for a "liberated" Bible would not be easy in an American setting, even removed a step or two from the power of New England's priests. Jefferson, especially, would enter into sharp conflict with the influence of the Anglican clergy of Virginia. He was acutely aware that many clergy portrayed him as nothing less than an atheistic infidel. So he consistently kept his own religious beliefs secret, hidden from public consumption and derision. This fact produced what I call a religious rhetoric of suppression—exhibited fundamentally in personal letters and his famous scissors-and-paste Bible, which consisted of selected extracts from the Gospels. Franklin, on the other hand, was more public with his religious beliefs. His literary effect on early America was profound, and he did not shy from including a view of the new distilled, nonecclesiastical religion that was fermenting in the Enlightenment. In this regard, he saw his task as one of drawing people to a religious view that transcended the dogmatic disputes of the priests. He undertook this effort most profoundly in his *Autobiography* and *Poor Richard's Almanack*. There is little doubt that he was a master craftsman in this rhetoric of persuasion. It is therefore a mistake to consider Jefferson and Franklin as anything less than genuine theologians: not theologians of the church, but theologians of the developing American mythos of exceptionality and mission. They were, so to say, priests of the Great Experiment, and their impact has been felt to our own day.

JEFFERSON AND THE RHETORIC OF SUPPRESSION

I am a real Christian, that is to say, a disciple of the doctrines of Jesus, very different from the Platonists, who call me infidel, and themselves Christians . . . while they draw all their characteristic dogmas from what its Author never said nor saw.[1]

In a letter dated 13 April 1820, Thomas Jefferson wrote to his protégé and secretary William Short,

> Among the sayings and discourses imputed to him [Jesus] by his biographers, I find many passages of fine imagination, correct morality, and of the most lovely benevolence; and others, again, of so much ignorance, so much absurdity, so much untruth, charlatanism and imposture, as to pronounce it impossible that such contradictions should have proceeded from the same being.[2]

---

[1]Jefferson to Charles Thomson, 9 January 1816, in Dickinson W. Adams, ed., *Jefferson's Extracts from the Gospels* (Princeton: Princeton University Press, 1983) 365.

[2]Jefferson to Short, 13 April 1820, in ibid., 392.

Sometime during the next four years Jefferson succeeded in creating a new Bible that he entitled *The Life and Morals of Jesus of Nazareth*; it was bereft of those contradictions that he had described to Short. This literally scissors-and-paste reconstruction of the Gospels in four languages (Greek, Latin, French, and English in parallel columns, modeled in part, perhaps, on his personal copy of Origen's *Hexapla*) was his second effort at freeing the "pure principles" of Jesus from the "artificial vestments in which they have been muffled by priests, who have travestied them into various forms, as instruments of riches and power to themselves." His first creation was completed in 1804, under the title *The Philosophy of Jesus of Nazareth*, but it had been "too hastily done" as he confided in a letter to Francis A. van der Kemp written in 1816.[3]

Jefferson's *Life and Morals of Jesus* raises a host of exegetical questions, but two are especially illuminating here. The most fundamental question to be asked of any text is, Why does it exist? What was Jefferson's intention in compiling the work? This question involves an inquiry into the birth of the text. The second question concerns the text in its maturity: What is the general structure of the composition, and what purpose and message does it reveal?

The first question—Why does the text exist?—must take into account Jefferson's unique scissors-and-paste methodology. He could simply have rewritten the account of Jesus in his own hand, with or without appropriate additions and alterations. But he chose not to do so. Instead he remained true not only to the literal words of the Gospels (with two very minor changes), but to the actual physical texture of the words as well. Why did he choose scissors and paste over his gifted pen? Although his correspondence does not offer a satisfactory answer to this question, a moment's reflection does reveal several obvious features of this approach. Most important, it retains something of the churchly Gospels, even as it alters greatly their content. What is it that is retained? The answer would seem to be the *authority* of the historical witness to Jesus that lay embedded in those Gospels. In other words, in the format that Jefferson chose, the book is not to be read simply as *his* view of Jesus, but as

---

[3]Jefferson to Francis A. van der Kemp, 25 April 1816, in ibid., 369.

the *true* Bible itself, displacing the one of the church. The author himself is masked.[4] He is replaced implicitly by the purified historical traditions preserved only imperfectly by the church. This is the first and most obvious indication that Jefferson intended something more for his creation than a book for his own night table.

Jefferson's use of four languages in his Bible meant that he intended it for the intellectual community rather than for the average citizen. Whatever else is achieved by including the original Greek and translations into three European languages, one fact is certain: this is a Bible rooted in human reason and not in the faith of the church. Dickinson Ward Adams has argued persuasively that the particular intellectual circle that Jefferson envisioned for the text was the University of Virginia. "His [Jefferson's] second compilation, in four languages, would inculcate all students at the University of Virginia in the principles of morality that supported Republicanism. In due course, there would spread from Charlottesville, over Virginia, and thence to the rest of the Republic those sociable and harmonizing principles."[5] For Jefferson, the University of Virginia was to be a citadel of reason, in stark contrast to the corrupt, priest-ridden church.[6] What institution other than the

---

[4]Dickinson Ward Adams has argued persuasively that Jefferson attempted to mask the intention of *The Philosophy of Jesus of Nazareth* because of the certain hostility that it would arouse. This was accomplished by a part of the subtitle that read, "for the use of the Indians unembarrassed with matters of fact or faith beyond their comprehension." Adams writes, "It may well have been then that Jefferson, seeking to make his compilation more acceptable, and still with the ideal of having the work published somehow, added the device of the sub-title." He adds, "The 'savages' Jefferson was most concerned about civilizing were the priests, the dissenting republicans, and all those who disturbed social harmony by their deformed reason and moral sense." See Adams, "Jefferson's Politics of Morality: The Purpose and Meaning of his Extracts from the Evangelists, *The Life and Morals of Jesus of Nazareth*" (Ph.D. dissertation, Brown University, 1970) 167, 170.

[5]Ibid., 242.

[6]Jefferson declared that the University of Virginia "will be based on the illimitable freedom of the human mind. For here we are not afraid to follow the truth wherever it may lead, nor to tolerate any error as long as reason is left free to combat it" (quoted in David B. Tyack, ed., *Turning Points in American Educational History*

university would be strong enough to face up to and finally overcome the power of the priests? The academic aura of his Bible shouted out the difference between it and the Bible of the church. It was not for believers who meekly submitted to church creed and doctrine. It was for those who had the courage to make up their own minds.[7] The variety of languages would give the scholar room to maneuver in order to catch the various nuances of Jesus' teaching.

Was this approach presumptuous? Of course it was. It could only have been conceived in the midst of a deeply felt hostility against the orthodox Christian tradition. Jefferson bore the brunt of as much criticism as any major political figure up until the present. Certainly a major object of that criticism was Jefferson's suspect religious views.[8] One who attacked Paul ("the first corruptor of the

---

[Blaisdell Publishing Co., 1967] 91). Rockne McCarthy, "Civil Religion in Early America," *Fides et Historia* 8 (Fall 1975): 27, writes, "His profound distaste for theology and the church led him not only to advocate Virginia's Bill for Religious Freedom, but also to found the University of Virginia as a non-sectarian alternative to Virginia's Anglican College of William and Mary."

[7]Jefferson wrote his nephew Peter Carr on 10 August 1787: "Read the Bible . . . as you would read Livy or Tacitus. The facts which are within the ordinary course of nature you will believe on the authority of the writer. . . . But those facts in the Bible which contradict the laws of nature, must be examined with more care, and under a variety of faces." Jefferson continued, "I forgot to observe when speaking of the New Testament that you should read all the histories of Christ, as well of those whom a council of ecclesiastics have decided for us to be Pseudo-evangelists, as those they named Evangelists, because these Pseudo-evangelists pretended to inspiration as much as the others, and you are to judge their pretensions by your own reason, and not by the reason of those ecclesiastics." Cf. Julian P. Boyd, ed., *The Papers of Thomas Jefferson* (Princeton: Princeton University Press, 1950) 15-17. James Lafayette Gurley, "Thomas Jefferson's Philosophy and Theology: As Related to His Political Principles, including Separation of Church and State" (Ph.D. dissertation, University of Michigan, 1975) 90, notes that for Jefferson, the Bible "must be examined critically and boldly, applying the same tests of literary and historical criticism as would be used in the examination of any other historical work."

[8]Jefferson wrote Joseph Priestley's son on 27 December 1804 that he had no objection if his "Syllabus" became publicly known, and added, "My wish was confined to the suppression of the Syllabus I sent him until the political passions

doctrines of Jesus"), Athanasius ("impious dogmatist"), John Calvin ("atheist"), and other venerable purveyors of Christian tradition in his correspondence could hardly expect immunity from public condemnation.[9] Even his lifelong membership in the Anglican church could not conceal his true convictions. Neither could his well-known reluctance to discuss his religious views openly.[10] Jefferson knew just how far his religion diverged from that of the church; he dared not publish *The Life and Morals of Jesus*. Any work on religion authored by Jefferson would have been anathema to the church—first simply because of its connection with Jefferson and, second, for its content. But the program followed in *The Life and Morals of Jesus* offered the best chance of overcoming the difficulties. For him, the new Bible he created was really the old authoritative Scripture harvested from the corrupt churchly Bible as wheat among the tares. It was "holy" and authoritative in the only real sense in which he could accept those words, namely, that it gave a true and reasonable picture of Jesus. According to Jefferson, most of the Bible of the church was antithetical to the teachings of Jesus. He sought, therefore, to displace the displacer. The American mythos, operating at the fundamental levels of cultural awareness, provided an environment in which Jefferson could produce a basic text that could strengthen the moral fiber of the new Republic.[11]

---

which have been kindled against me shall be so far subsided as to admit its being read with candid & just dispositions. But that will not be during my life." Quoted by Dickinson Adams, "Jefferson's Politics of Morality," 165, who lists the original manuscript as his source. Adams notes, "It is clear that he [Jefferson] felt that his religious views would be attacked merely because they were his, not so much because of the views themselves" (165).

[9]One of the best accounts of attacks on Jefferson is documented in Fred C. Luebke, "The Origins of Thomas Jefferson's Anti-Clericalism," *Church History* 32 (1963): 346-52.

[10]See A. Arnold Wettstein, "Religionless Religion in the Letters and Papers from Monticello," *Religion in Life* 45 (1976): 152-60, esp. 156-57.

[11]On 9 January 1816 Jefferson wrote to Charles Thomson, "*I* am a *real Christian*, that is to say, a disciple of the doctrine of Jesus, very different from the Platonists, who call *me* infidel and *themselves* Christians and preachers of the Gospel, while

The structure of *The Life and Morals of Jesus* helps to underscore Jefferson's conviction that Jesus' message was distorted from the moment of its utterance. For throughout the major subdivisions of his account we find Jesus constantly challenged and confronted by the religious leaders of his own Jewish tradition. Jefferson's evaluation of the Judaism of Jesus' day is even harsher, if possible, than his judgment of the Christian impostors who followed Jesus.

> The office of reformer of the superstitions of a nation is ever dangerous. Jesus had to walk on the perilous confines of reason and religion; and a step to the right or left might place him within the grip of the priests of the superstition, a bloodthirsty race as cruel and remorseless as the Being whom they represented as the family God of Abraham, of Isaac and of Jacob, and the local God of Israel.[12]

The enemies Jesus faced were the religionists of his day, and his conflict with them determined, for Jefferson, the major stages of his life and teachings.

The overall corpus of *The Life and Morals of Jesus* divides almost to the line into three equal parts, which for convenience may be entitled:

    I. The Advent of Jesus and His Message
   II. The Message in Conflict with Jewish Religion
  III. The Message of the End Time

As the centerpiece of each of these subdivisions stand large blocks of material lifted almost without interruption from Matthew and Luke. In the first subdivision we find the Sermon on the Mount, essentially in its entirety. In the second, Jefferson follows the teachings, warnings, and parables found in Luke 14-18, omitting the

---

they draw all their characteristic dogmas from what its author never said nor saw. They have compounded from the heathen mysteries a system beyond the comprehension of man, of which the great reformer of the vicious ethics and deism of the Jews, were he to return on earth, would not recognize one feature"; in Adams, *Jefferson's Extracts*, 365.

[12]Jefferson to Short, 4 August 1820, in ibid., 396-97.

miracle stories that he found unpalatable. Finally, in the third section, the concluding events recorded in Matthew 21-27 concerning Jesus in Jerusalem, specifically, his discussions and controversies with the Pharisees and Sadducees, his eschatological discourses and parables, and his passion narrative make up the central thread.[13]

The opening section consists of the *sayings* of Jesus and the so-called parables of advent. The hinge verse dividing the first section from the second is statement enough of Jefferson's view concerning the public reception of this inaugural period of Jesus' life. That verse (John 7:1) says, "After these things Jesus walked in Galilee for he would not walk in Jewry, because the Jews sought to kill him." The most intriguing instance of Jefferson's reconstruction of the Gospel accounts in order to emphasize the hostility between Jesus and Jewish religious leaders occurs at the conclusion of the Sermon on the Mount. In Matthew's account, the Sermon is followed by the story of the Cleansing of the Leper, the Healing of the Centurion's Servant, the Healing of Peter's Mother-in-law, and the Healing of the Sick at Evening. Jefferson replaces these events with a summary of the Sermon, using the brief call to those who labor and are heavy-laden (Matt. 11:28-30), and then the narration of the controversies surrounding the woman with the ointment in the house of a Pharisee (Luke 7:36-46, omitting Jesus' forgiveness of her sins).

Controversy with the Jewish religious leaders only intensifies in the second section of Jefferson's Bible. From a literary perspective, emphasis now falls upon the so-called "parables of reversal" and exemplary stories such as the Rich Man and Lazarus, the Prodigal Son, and the conclusions to the Lukan centerpiece, the Pharisee and the Publican.[14] Here, at the very heart of his Bible—and the po-

---

[13]Unlike Dickinson Adams, who emphasizes the life of Jesus as a moral example in *The Life and Morals of Jesus*, my analysis reveals that the message of Jesus takes precedence over the life of Jesus. It is precisely at the point when that message came into conflict with the "priests" of Israel that the person of Jesus becomes of particular interest to Jefferson. It was not, primarily, Jesus as a moral example that attracted Jefferson, but Jesus as a reformer.

[14]On parables of reversal, see John Dominic Crossan, *In Parables* (Harper & Row, 1973) 53-78.

Charles Mabee

sition is very significant—Jefferson follows the theology of Luke and most likely that of Jesus himself in saying that truth is not as it appears in the world. In fact, truth can only be known in a paradoxical way, and is best expressed in parabolic forms of paradoxical aphorism. From this perspective, those religious officials who appear to propound the true faith are seen to be truly false teachers. The parable creates what recent New Testament scholarship calls a "creative disruption" in the mind of the hearer.[15] Thus the message of Jesus overturns the teachings of the "priests" of Israel, and shows them to be hindrances to truth rather than guides. This function of parable has very close analogy to the general thrust of Jefferson's entire Bible. Just as Jesus reverses the position of the Pharisees, so too does the work of Jefferson reveal the utter falsity of what he terms the teaching of the "Christian Platonists." It is not the giants of Christian tradition who offer the way to God, but those who, like Jefferson himself, walk the fine line between reason and religion.

Of course, the conflict between Jesus and Jewish "priests" comes to a head in the third, and concluding, subdivision. The opening verse of this section is an obvious introduction to the final climactic events of Jesus' life: "And when they drew nigh unto Jerusalem . . ." (Matthew 21:1). Jefferson's portrayal of the final confrontation between Jesus and the Israelite "priests" basically follows the course of Matthew 21:27, with appropriate deletions and additions from other Gospels. For example, the first insertion he makes after the opening of Matthew 21 comes from John 12:19-24, which begins, "The Pharisees therefore said among themselves, Perceive ye how ye prevail nothing? Behold the world is gone after him." Was it envy that generated the last events of Jesus' life? Perhaps that is Jefferson's diagnosis of what he believed to be priestly malignity. Literary investigations reveal continued disputations with the Pharisees and Sadducees, eschatological discourses and parables, and the passion narrative. Now Pharisaic hostility evi-

---

[15]See William A. Beardslee, "Parable, Proverb, and Koan," *Semeia* 12 (1978): 172.

dent from the very beginning moves from foreboding threat to the actual death of Jesus, recorded as accusation, trial, and execution.

In light of his rationalistic bias, it may come as somewhat of a surprise to learn that Jefferson retains a goodly amount of the eschatological discourses of Matthew 24-25. It is common to conceive of *The Life and Morals of Jesus* as a "demythologized" New Testament—a perspective difficult to maintain in light of certain of these discourses.[16] A careful check of those verses that Jefferson retained and omitted suggests that he was not primarily concerned with demythologizing the New Testament. Rather we might term his method one of "declericalization." Any passage that promotes the perspective or the interests of priests is disqualified. The tone of much of Matthew 24-25, aggressively attacking the Jewish religious establishment, is right on target from Jefferson's perspective. In fact, the ultimate alteration in the world order that Jesus here proclaims fittingly concludes the idea of reversal highlighted in the previous section. For Jefferson, the essential apocalyptic component in Jesus' teachings becomes an expression of Jefferson's conviction that reasoned truth will prevail in the end. The priests may have their power and influence now, but there will come a day when the world will see them for what they are. And if Jesus is first rightly understood by large numbers of his followers on American soil, with Jefferson himself at the forefront, then so be it!

By now it should be clear that the major alteration that Jefferson makes in the churchly Gospels is a profoundly heightened sense of the hostility to be found between Jesus and the Jewish "priests." Such a blatant disruption in the original text demands interpreta-

---

[16]According to Fesperman, "Jefferson's Bible," 81, "Jefferson engaged in a 'demythologization' which is not as drastic as more modern exercises by that name but which he felt was not only justifiable but necessary for enlightened religion." The problem, without any real solution, is raised by Gurley: "While Jefferson *intended* to strip the Gospel of all miracles and traces of Jesus' supernatural character, he left remnants of these elements in his *Extracts*" (italics added), "Thomas Jefferson's Philosophy," 109. Is Gurley suggesting that Jefferson was not true to his own intention? It is more likely that Jefferson saw a role for religion independent of, yet in concert with human reason, especially as he entered the maturity of his later years.

tion. In a letter to the Reverend Charles Clay, rector of St. Anne's Parish in Albemarle County, Virginia, Jefferson confirms the suspicion of the exegete.

> I abuse the priests, indeed, who have so much abused the pure and holy doctrines of their master, and who have laid me under no obligations of reticence as to the tricks of their trade. The genuine system of Jesus, and the artificial structures they have erected to make him the instrument of wealth, power, and preeminence to themselves, are as distinct things in my view as light and darkness: and, while I have classed them with soothsayers and necromancers, I place him among the greatest of the reformers of morals, and scourges of priestcraft that has ever existed. They felt him as such, and never rested until they had silenced him by death. *But his heresies against Judaism prevailing in the long run, the priests have tacked about, and rebuilt upon them the temple which he destroyed, as splendid, as profitable, and as imposing as that.*

A few lines later he concludes, "I consider reformation and redress as desperate, and abandon them to the Quixotism of more enthusiastic minds."[17] The view from Monticello was that the Pharisees of old had not been destroyed by Jesus, but had merely changed dress and formed the Christian church itself. In the prophetic and apologetic spirit of a true devotee of Jesus, Jefferson fought back with the most powerful tool he could conceive of as a lay follower of his great moral teacher and fellow reformer. Just as Jesus had scourged the priesthood of ancient Israel, he would scourge the priests of Christianity with their own authoritative Scriptures. Just as Jesus had reduced all the priestly law codes to Two Great Commandments, Jefferson would rescue the simple and sublime teaching of Jesus from the machinations of the priests who had come after him. The "parables of reversal" in Luke with their paradoxical character would be the heart of his indictment of the church.

A simple dictionary definition of paradox is "a statement contrary to received opinion." So one might well characterize *The Life*

---

[17]Jefferson to Clay, 29 January 1815, in Adams, *Jefferson's Extracts*, 363; italics added.

and Morals of Jesus. It represents a statement of a priestless Christianity. Jefferson knew that the hostility such a work would provoke, particularly among the priests themselves, would be more than he could comfortably endure during his years of retirement at Monticello. As a result, he never attempted to have the work published. But it was a Bible that would lie "in deposit" until such time after his death that enough Americans would have progressed to its reasoned religious perspective. It was a work that he hoped would stand vigilantly for all time against the tendencies of usurpation on the part of the priests. In that sense, it should rank with his political documents as a primary exhibit of the Jeffersonian mind. He fervently hoped for America that the tyranny of the priest (whether Pharisaic or Christian) that had brought about the death of Jesus might finally be over. Only then could true Christianity take its rightful place as the moral backbone of the nation. The American mythos, with its emphasis on cultural exceptionality and worldwide mission, had transcended its Puritan origins. It was now moving into the mainstream of cultural consciousness and formation.

FRANKLIN
AND THE RHETORIC
OF SEDUCTION

As to Jesus of Nazareth, . . . I think the System of Morals and his Religion, as he left them to us, the best the World ever saw or is likely to see; but I apprehend it has received various corrupting Changes, and I have, with most of the present Dissenters in England, some Doubts as to his Divinity; tho' it is a question I do not dogmatize upon, having never studied it, and think it needless to busy myself with it now, when I expect soon an Opportunity of knowing the Truth with less Trouble.[1]

Benjamin Franklin's opposition to any and all expressions of religious dogmatism typified the Enlightenment, exhibiting precisely what Sidney Mead termed the "Religion of the Republic." Because of the widespread effect of Franklin's work on the American psyche, it is important to understand the strategy he followed in combating narrowly conceived religious expression and to evaluate the extent of the influence of his religious views on his thought. But

---

[1]Franklin to Ezra Stiles, 9 March 1790, in Albert Henry Smythe, ed., *The Works of Benjamin Franklin*, vol. 10 (New York: Macmillan, 1905-1907) 83-85.

first it is necessary to establish the context of Franklin's hostility to confessional Christianity. Only then will we be able to see how his strategy exceeded the literary conventions of his day, and to draw out some of the implications of his rhetoric for his proposed reform of (Reformed) theology.

Early in the *Autobiography*, Franklin writes,

> My Father's little library consisted chiefly of books in polemic Divinity, most of which I read. I have since regretted, that at a time when I had such a Thirst for Knowledge, more proper Books had not fallen in my Way, since it was now resolv'd I should not be a Clergyman.[2]

If there were other books in divinity in his father's library aside from the polemical kind, we do not hear of them in the *Autobiography*. No doubt Franklin found it quite easy to confuse the terms "polemic" and "divinity." But rather than undertake a search for more level-headed approaches to religious issues, he chose to channel his intellectual pursuits in other directions. He once gave an English correspondent standing instructions to send him regularly as they were published "such new pamphlets as are worth reading on any subject (religious controversy excepted)."[3] At times his private correspondence demonstrates his holding at arms-length religious teachings that others would take in all seriousness. For example, in a letter to Madame d'Hardancourt Brillon, written while he was an American representative in France, he confesses to "Coveting my Neighbor's Wife," and adds,

> And now I am consulting you upon a Case of Conscience, I will mention the Opinion of a certain Father of the Church, which I find myself willing to adopt, tho' I am not sure it is orthodox. It is this, that the most effectual Way to get rid of a certain Temptation, is, as

----

[2]Leonard W. Labaree, ed., *The Autobiography of Benjamin Franklin* (New Haven: Yale University Press, 1964) 58. All subsequent references are to this edition with the abbreviation *Auto*.

[3]Quoted in Leonard W. Labaree, "Franklin and the Presbyterians," *Journal of the Presbyterian Historical Society* 35 (1957): 220.

often as it returns, to comply with and satisfy it. Pray instruct me how far I may venture to practice upon this Principle?[4]

Franklin obviously saw himself dealing with more serious matters than religious orthodoxy. In fact, his lighthearted, airy indifference to it was the external manifestation of a deeper, underlying weariness. An aphorism found in *Poor Richard's Almanack* (November 1743) perhaps best summarizes his feelings.

Many a long dispute among Divines may be thus abridged,
It is so: It is not so.
It is so: It is not so.

The problem Franklin wanted to address in the new American setting above all others was not the issue of religious truth per se, but the need for religion to produce good citizens. The narrowness of most religious dogma hindered the moral effectiveness of religion at its best. This is why Franklin spends so little effort in telling others what to believe, but so much time in pointing out those areas that stifle growth and development. For Franklin, it is clear that the new American religious "type" would be one freed from the narrowness of the past. He would be the heir to the promised rationality of the Enlightenment. More precisely, he would be the antitypical American version of this universal Enlightenment type.

Franklin claims that his upbringing in a confessional Christian context is the source of his misgivings about the inadequacies of existing ecclesiastical doctrine.

I had been religiously educated as a Presbyterian; and tho' some of the Dogmas of that Persuasion, such as the Eternal Decrees of God, Election, Reprobation, etc. appear'd to me unintelligible, others doubtful, and I early absented myself from the Public Assemblies of the Sect, Sunday being my Studying-Day. . . .

The key terms in this text are "Dogmas," "Persuasion," and "sect."

---

[4]Leonard W. Labaree and Whitfield J. Bell, Jr., eds., *Mr. Franklin: A Selection from His Personal Letters* (New Haven: Yale University Press, 1956) 43.

They pinpoint his basic quarrel with the Reformed tradition of his day, namely, that it tended to lose sight of the end of religious practice (moral edification), and was stymied at the means (sectarian identity). He illustrates this point with reference to a Presbyterian minister whom he encountered during his early years in Philadelphia.

> . . . his discourses were chiefly either polemic arguments, or explications of the peculiar doctrines of our sect, and were all to me very dry, uninteresting, and unedifying since not a single moral principle was inculcated or enforc'd, their aim seeming to be rather to make us Presbyterians than good citizens.[5]

On the other hand, the *Autobiography* informs us that Franklin later ("about the year 1734") did find a Presbyterian minister in Philadelphia who was more to his liking, a certain Hemphill from Ireland. He writes, "I became one of his constant Hearers, his Sermons pleasing me, as they had little of the dogmatical kind, but inculcated strongly the Practice of Virtue."[6] The Presbyterian Synod soon found Hemphill guilty of preaching doctrines "Unsound and Dangerous, contrary to the sacred Scriptures and our excellent Confession and Catechisms."[7] Franklin became his strong partisan throughout the ordeal, and upon his defeat "quitted the Congregation, never joining it after, tho' I continu'd many Years my Subscription for the Support of its Ministers."[8] It had been a battle that captured the essence of Franklin's relationship to the church.

His opposition to Reformed theology is also illustrated in his correspondence. One letter contains a parable in which Franklin

---

[5]*Auto*, 145-47.

[6]Ibid., 167ff.

[7]Quoted by permission from Paul Zall in his new edition of the *Autobiography* to be published by Norton. A detailed account of the views of Hemphill can be found in the letter of one of his opponents by the name of Obadiah Jenkins to a friend. Cf. Jenkins, "Remarks Upon the Defence of the Reverend Mr. Hemphill's Observations: In a Letter to a Friend" (Philadelphia: Bradford, 1735).

[8]*Auto*, 169.

imagines a man at the gates of heaven and applying for entrance on
the ground that he was a Presbyterian. "What is that?" St. Peter
asked, and when told he answered, "We don't have any here." The
astonished man mentioned different sects only to be rebuffed with
the news that there were none of these persuasions in heaven. Finally, the man saw his wife through the gate and claimed that if she
was there he should be too, for they were of the same religion on
earth. "Oh," said St. Peter, "Why didn't you say that you were a
Christian, to begin with?"[9]

Obviously, Presbyterianism and Christianity were not synonymous
terms. Neither, of course, were any other forms of particularized
religion.[10] Franklin's great respect for the Dunkers, for example,
was based on their refusal to reduce religious experience to doctrine.[11] There is no question that his refusal to engage himself actively in the religious life of his own Reformed tradition stemmed
not from its more general tenets but from the dogmatism that, he
believed, characterized it.

The common ground between Franklin and the churches lay in
their moral teachings. He applauded moral instruction when he
saw it, and he lamented its lack when he believed a cold, ineffective

---

[9]Paul L. Ford, *The Many-Sided Franklin* (New York: Century, 1899) 156-57.

[10]He writes in the *Autobiography* concerning those principles that he deemed essential for all the religions we had in our country. "I respected them all, tho' with
different degrees of Respect as I found them more or less mixed with other Articles
which without an Tendency to inspire, promote or confirm Morality, serv'd prin-
cipally to divide us and make us unfriendly to one another" (146).

[11]The Dunker Michael Welfare (Wohlfahrt) explained to Franklin that "we fear
that if we should once print our Confession of Faith, we should feel ourselves as if
bound and confin'd by it, and perhaps be unwilling to receive farther Improvement; and our Successors still more so, as conceiving what we their Elders and
Founders had done, to be something sacred, never to be departed from." Franklin
responded, "This Modesty in a Sect is perhaps a singular Instance in the History
of Mankind, every other Sect supposing itself in Possession of all Truth, and that
those who differ are so far in the Wrong: Like a Man travelling in foggy Weather:
Those at some Distance before him on the Road he sees wrapt up in the Fog as any
of them" (*Auto*, 190-91).

doctrine had been substituted for it. But he was not content to stand on the sidelines, merely observing and criticizing the failures of the existing moral teachers, the clergy. Like Jefferson, yet in his own inimitable style, he sought to supplant their counterproductive efforts with his own moral teachings. In his two major literary creations, the *Autobiography* and *Poor Richard's Almanack*, Franklin succeeded in broadening the arena of ethical teaching far beyond that achieved by the theologians. The massive impact of those two works stems quite naturally from their general readability and their relevance to life in the New World. Franklin's rhetorical success in stretching the forms of the literary genre he employed—the autobiography and the almanac—was directly related to this ability to gain a hearing for his moral teachings and to establish an antitype of the American self that was capable of challenging in his and succeeding generations the dominant Puritan image.

The first paragraph of the *Autobiography*, set in the context of a note to his son, gives the ostensible purpose of the book.

> Having emerg'd from the Poverty and Obscurity in which I was born and bred, to a State of Affluence and some Degree of Reputation in the World, and having gone so far thro' Life with a considerable Share of Felicity, the conducing Means I made use of, which, with the Blessing of God so well succeeded, my Posterity may like to know, as they may find some of them suitable to their own Situations, and therefore fit to be imitated.

Obviously, the personal tone of this introduction is designed to gain the reader's affections and is a carefully considered rhetorical device. However, much later in the book, we find the genuine statement of Franklin's intentions that does not deny the opening paragraph so much as unfold out of it.

> In this Piece it was my Design to explain and enforce this Doctrine, that vicious Actions are not hurtful because they are forbidden, but forbidden because they are hurtful, the Nature of Man alone consider'd: That it was therefore every one's Interest to be virtuous, who wish'd to be happy even in this World. And I . . . have endeav-

oured to convince young Persons, that no Qualities were so likely
to make a poor Man's Fortune as those of Probity and Integrity.[12]

Whatever Franklin's other personal or underlying intentions were
in writing the book, this is the proper starting point for studying it
as it now stands.[13] Now we learn that the book is not written simply
for his own son, but for all young persons in order to show them
the virtues of "probity and integrity." It is obvious that he has chosen to reach beyond the historical feature of autobiography as a literary genre toward something more like the German *Bildungsroman*
or psychological novel. It is not that his life is to be viewed as a subject of general interest or amusement, but it is one to be imitated by
the young (and immature). It established a new, nondogmatic
American religious type, in harmony with the prevailing American
mythos. That the church had obscured the lives of its founder,
prophets, apostles, and saints with religious dogmas is presup-
posed. Franklin was bold enough to propose his own life typolog-
ically as an alternative to religious doctrine. His life revealed that
the moral substratum of successful living did not depend on adherence to "the distinguishing tenets of any particular sect."[14]

Just as in the case of the *Autobiography*, Franklin's first edition of
Poor Richard's Almanack (1733) gives the reader an immediate indication of rhetorical strategy.

> I might in this place attempt to gain thy Favour, by declaring that I
> write Almanacks with no other View than that of the publick Good;
> but in this I should not be sincere; and Men are now adays too wise
> to be deceiv'd by Pretences how specious soever. The plain Truth
> of the matter is, I am excessive poor, and my Wife, good Woman,

---

[12]Ibid., 43, 158.

[13]Melvin H. Buxbaum, *Benjamin Franklin and the Zealous Presbyterians* (University Park: Pennsylvania State University Press, 1975) 2, refers to a "propagandistic
intention" in the *Autobiography* that Franklin conceived of as "a public relations
piece not only for himself but for America, and in developing the hero of his mem-
oirs he created a typical American of the kind he wanted to see settle in his
country."

[14]*Auto*, 157.

> is, I tell her, excessive proud; she cannot bear, she says, to sit spin-
> ning in her Shift of Tow, while I do nothing but gaze at the Stars;
> and has threatened more than once to burn all my Books and Rat-
> tling-Traps (as she calls my Instruments) if I do not make some
> profitable Use of them for the good of my Family. The Printer has
> offer'd me some considerable share of the Profits, and I have thus
> begun to comply with my Dame's desire.

As in the *Autobiography*, Franklin ostensibly points to the family as
the locus of his motivation for writing. Rather than a plan of life to
be imitated by his son, here it is simply the poverty of his family
that propels Poor Richard into the almanac business. It is a humor-
ous statement meant to capture the reader's attention and imagination. In his supposed candidness with the reader, Franklin is
characteristically employing a rhetorical device that operates on
two levels. In a literal sense, it is true, of course, that a scholar
ought to make some "profitable Use" of his "Books and Rattling-
Traps," and that poverty is an unacceptable mode of existence even
for one devoted to the life of the intellect. On a deeper level, the
candid insight that he so openly shares concerning the inner dynamics of his private life establishes an intimate bond that breaks
through the objective framework of the almanac genre. Almanacs
traditionally contained objective, useful, public information—a ca-
lendric chart of the movement of the heavenly bodies, an opera-
tional schedule of the courts, geographical distances between
points of common interest, and the like. But from the start, Franklin's almanac has the character of a personal confession. This is to
be a work from which one can learn not only about the world but
also about oneself. What could be more in stark contrast to the dogmatic, impersonal pronouncements of the churches? Here was
moral teaching to be trusted because it was fashioned by an honest
private citizen, rather than by the deceptive clergy.

Interpreted against this background, and defined in his own
terms, Franklin ought to be conceived of as a religious thinker of
the highest order in the American experience. Certainly his work
indicates a carefully thought out method or strategy for persuading
the public of the benefits of ethical life. It is of fundamental importance to this strategy that he would promote morality outside the

context of ecclesiastical religion rather than within it. We should not hastily conclude that this choice made him a heretic. Heresy is a religious concept, and because it is defined by those who lay claim to orthodoxy, it frequently denies the complex levels of meaning in any given religious formulation. The concept itself is dogmatic and represents precisely the type of religious thinking that Franklin was attempting to transcend. Just as the art of his most popular works was meant to operate on various levels, depending on the degree of literalness that the reader brought to them, so too ought religious instruction be multivalent.

In the absence of the natural authority that accompanied ecclesiastical creeds and doctrine, Franklin had to come up with an adequate substitute if he hoped to make a contribution to the well-being of his fellow citizens. In order to give his ideas a chance of acceptance, he early applied himself to the study of rhetoric, the general improvement of his language, and the Socratic method.[15] Of these, it was particularly his mastery of rhetoric that enabled him to make a significant impact on the American mind.

Among the many aspects of Franklin's rhetoric that deserve attention, the disarming simplicity that characterizes his style is particularly noteworthy, and is not without theological implications. Life is not as simple as it is made out to be in the *Autobiography* or the almanacs. The possibility that it will seem so is the constant danger of wisdom literature (including much of that in the Bible) or wisdomlike narrative, such as autobiography or *Bildungsroman*. But it would be a mistake to conclude from Franklin's writings that he was a victim of philosophic naiveté.

Franklin's simple style was self-consciously utilitarian. The directness that characterizes the *Autobiography* and the shape of Poor Richard's aphorisms is at the heart of Franklin's genius. Of course, an economical writing style possesses an inherent quality of intellectual persuasiveness and seduction. And if Franklin wished to gain an audience for his moral teachings, he would need to be persuasive.

---

[15]Ibid., 61ff.

Simply to speak the truth would hardly be sufficient. He was entering an arena dominated at that time by the church, so he would need to counterbalance its authority in some way. He decided to let the public choose between ecclesiastical casuistry and the seductive rhetoric of honest simplicity. He realized that one of the primary functions of the intellect is to remove unnecessary obstacles to insight. That in itself was an insight that escaped many members of the clergy in his day. Franklin came to believe that the complexity of their doctrines and the elaborate ways they glossed over the simple truths of the Bible conspired to hinder the church from guiding its members to a virtuous life. He saw the clergy falling victim all too often to the temptation of molding people in its own image, rather than in the image of the God it claimed to represent.

Franklin's battle with the church captured the essence of the philosophic implications of the new world vis-à-vis the old. The church as it stood in his day was a casualty of the old European intellectual traditions. Its doctrines did not liberate, rather they enslaved. This oppressive character of the church simply could not be tolerated by Franklin as he addressed the culture of the Republic in its formative years.

In his transcendence of the heresy/orthodoxy categories proclaimed by the church, Franklin produces a foretaste for perhaps the single most important theological issue to result from the experience of American pluralism: how can any single dogmatic viewpoint be advanced by a given tradition within a pluralistic religious environment? Unless that tradition accepts a certain degree of relativity in its convictions, it finds itself splintered off from the others in an unhealthy posture of self-defense. In such a situation, one worries about Reformed theology (or the like) to the neglect of Christian theology. Of course, the other side of the coin is that one's religious tradition may venture too far in the direction of relativity, blandly affirming that all traditions are equally true. Franklin correctly saw this great problem of American public religion. How could American churches continue to proclaim the oneness of truth in the face of their existence in mutual exclusivity? He did not finally answer that question for those who continued to labor within the church, although he pointed to a solution of sorts in his distil-

lation of religion into morality. This was a "utilitarian" sort of answer that was pervasive among Enlightenment thinkers. A
utilitarian approach did admit to an intellectual toleration. In June
1772 Franklin published "A Letter on Religious Toleration" in an
English newspaper.

> If we look back into history for the character of the present sects in
> Christianity, we shall find few that have not, in their turns, been
> persecutors and complainers of persecution. The primitive Chris-
> tian thought persecution extremely wrong in the pagans, but prac-
> ticed it on one another. The first Protestants of the Church of
> England blamed persecution in the Romish Church, but practiced
> it against the Puritans; these found it wrong in the bishops, but fell
> into the same practice both here and in New England.—To account
> for this we should remember that the doctrine of *toleration* was not
> then known, or had not prevailed in the world.[16]

It would have been easier, perhaps, for Franklin to have abandoned the church as a lost cause and to have genuinely labored for
its demise. Instead, to the perceptive eye, his work has more the
character of reform, designed to shake the church free from idola-
trous dogmatism. Presbyterianism was not the answer; a proper
Christianity grounded in the New World mythos might well be.
The fictions of his rhetorical style were tied to the hopes and aspirations of the newly born American imagination. What better time
and place to launch a well-laden ship of moral goods, freed from
the dogmatic machinations of the clergy that were "comic profound," unlike the ecclesiastical pronouncements.

Therefore, in Franklin, as well as in Jefferson, we witness the intellectual strivings for a new religious archetype in America. It represents essentially the same mentality as the traditional type-
antitype structure of the Puritans, only now it is set in the broader
context of the goals and aspirations of the Enlightenment. This dialectic between the scriptural Puritan thinkers and the natural phi-
losophers of the Enlightenment established the interior dialectic of

---

[16]Printed in Herbert W. Schneider, ed., *Benjamin Franklin: The Autobiography and
Selections from His Other Writings* (New York: The Liberal Arts Press, 1953) 180.

the American mythos. All who followed would need to confront this dialectic if they wanted to understand the meaning of the New World. Herman Melville and Robert Pirsig have done so in especially provocative ways.

PART III

THE LIBERATION OF THE UNIVERSAL FROM AMERICAN RELIGION

M any thoughtful interpreters of the American experience who labored during and after the American Renaissance bear witness to a deepening distortion of the mythos of exceptionality and
mission. The promised results of an unfettered reason, which had so
attracted Jefferson and Franklin, were beginning to be perceived as hope-
lessly naive. As we might expect, many of the strongest critics were men
of letters. The Renaissance period itself brought tensions to a head.
While it could produce the Great Experiment's singer of tales in Whit-
man, the dark underbelly of the mythos began to be manifest most powerfully in Hawthorne. Hawthorne utilized the typological traditions
native to his New England heritage in radically new ways. Cracks in
the surface of the mythos were beginning to develop, and opportunity
existed for the courageous to plummet its depths. It was left to Hawthorne's greatest admirer, Herman Melville, to dive the deepest of all.
In the process, he produced nothing less than the sacred text critiquing
the mythos—Moby Dick. From his time until our own, the path to any
theology of the American experience runs through this text.

Melville's crucial insight was that the American mythos, rather
than manifesting the reality of the human condition, had in fact obscured

it. The universal, scientific guidelines of the Great Experiment established by the founding figures had become a new guise by which elusive truth could hide itself. As Melville began to see, science distorts and artificializes the natural world in the process of its partial revelation. The metaphor of scientific experiment in the context of American social thought was subject to the same sort of distortion. Americans, in other words, simply by virtue of adopting the universal language of science, could not exempt themselves from the particularities of their human existence. The reality that was "out there" in the world would not be so easily tamed. In the process, Americans were becoming alarmingly distorted, as their attempt to remake the world in the image of the received mythos was actually cutting them off from the wellsprings of human existence. The Christian religion, which all too frequently allowed itself to be seduced by the mythmakers, offered little hope for needed reforms. In contradistinction to the bulk of ecclesiastical theologians who whitewashed their religion with a soothing portrayal of Jesus, Melville would take his religion straight by delving into the complexities of the Old Testament. It seems that the church's distortions of Jesus had neutralized the New Testament and prepared the way for the seething critique of the American mythos that Melville proposed.

Hawthorne and Melville are not the only American interpreters to venture into the inner darkness of the cultural mythos. Poe, for example, found his own inimitable way of dealing with the tragic side of the American predicament. The next generation would produce the towering figure of Mark Twain, who ventured from coast to coast in producing several volumes of epic dark humor. In the twentieth century, the pessimism surrounding the mythos would become more mature and pervasive. Indeed, it finally even became fashionable in literary circles to acknowledge the early prophetic genius of Melville himself. Such works as Fitzgerald's *The Great Gatsby* in the 1920s, and Kesey's *One Flew*

Over the Cuckoo's Nest in our own generation certainly depict the American mythic hero turned sour in the twentieth century. All of these works carry extraordinary theological power and significance. However, a novel appeared in 1974 that seems to have addressed the problem of American mythic consciousness in a singular way—Robert Pirsig's *Zen and the Art of Motorcycle Maintenance*. Its title might belie the book's underlying philosophical, aesthetic, and finally, theological sensitivity, but I am convinced that a careful reading reveals a unique literary achievement. For that reason, I have given it a prominent role in this introductory study in American biblical hermeneutics.

The novel makes very little explicit reference to Judeo-Christian theological categories. And I believe that very fact is instructive in the theological analysis of our time. That such a penetrating look at who we are—what our fundamental problems are—rarely refers to our biblical heritage is itself of profound theological significance. Again, as the nonecclesiastical aspect of the American mythic tradition has always maintained, the problem is not with the teachings of Jesus, it is with the communities founded in his name.

Of all the potentially provocative literary works that are relevant to the problem of the theology of American mythic religion, none are more appropriate than Melville's *Moby-Dick* and Pirsig's *Zen and the Art of Motorcycle Maintenance*. Each addresses the question of the sacredness of life in an explicitly philosophical as well as literary way. As genuine philosophical sophistication is rare in America, especially among those sensitive to the problems of the American mythos, both these works embody a seldom-seen transition from the aesthetic to the philosophical-theological realms. Therefore, I have chosen to introduce these works into a hermeneutical dialogue with parts of the Bible that appear most suggestive. Certainly my work in this regard approaches untested theological shores. It is quite possible to attempt the same kind of hermeneutical dialogue with other literary and biblical texts. In fact, the work that follows is meant to encourage just this sort of thing. While I am not trying to establish yet another method of biblical criticism, it is quickly apparent that I am trying to distinguish American biblical hermeneutics from the various forms of literary criticism—whether inside or outside the field of biblical studies.

The work of hermeneutics is intrinsically theological (or philosophical); it is, in other words, a quest for *meaning*. Meaning can come from many different directions, and result from the application of a number of different methods. Therefore, in the selection that follows, the heart of this book, I will attempt to utilize the work of American literary mythologists to draw out new meaning from biblical texts. If the Bible is inherently hermeneutical, as I believe it is, then logically each new generation of humans should find new insights in that ancient literary source. Finally, I hope to show that the best way to read the Bible is to begin by reading ourselves.

THE HERMENEUTICS
OF DISPLACEMENT

. . .though directly from the Latin word for white, all Christian priests derive the name of one part of their sacred vesture, the alb or tunic, worn beneath the cassock; and though among the holy pomps of the Romish faith, white is specially employed in the celebration of the Passion of our Lord; though in the Vision of St. John, white robes are given to the redeemed, and the four and twenty elders stand clothed in white before the great white throne, and the Holy One that sitteth there white like wool; yet for all these accumulated associations, with whatever is sweet, and honorable, and sublime, there yet lurks an elusive something in the innermost idea of this hue, which strikes more of panic to the soul than that redness which affrights in blood.[1]

• Melville's White Truth •

A book about words ("Etymology" and "Extracts"). Like its title, the book *Moby-Dick or, the Whale* is divided into two parts. These are (1)

---

[1]Herman Melville, *Moby-Dick or, The Whale*, ed. Charles Feidelson, Jr. (Indianapolis: Bobbs-Merrill, 1964) 254-55. All page citations are to this edition.

the opening sections entitled "Etymology" and "Extracts" followed by (2) chapter headings numbered 1-135 and a brief epilogue. Just as the name Moby-Dick gives identity and meaning to the whale in the title, the curious sections "Etymology" and "Extracts" name and establish the meaning of the story. Without the particular name Moby-Dick (that is, unless the identity of Moby-Dick is known from the outset by Ahab), the entire account is simply an adventure story. It is the known identity of Moby-Dick that gives the story theological meaning. In similar fashion, "Etymology" and "Extracts" give the story theological depth. They tell us immediately that the book is not to be read simply as a story: it is one that is meant to be interpreted. If we wish to call it a story at all, it is a story about language. *Etymology*, of course, traces words back to their origin and makes our understanding of them more profound by uncovering nuances that are otherwise lost through the passage of time. Similarly, Melville's etymological introduction indicates that the key to the novel is a deeper understanding of old words (and concepts). This means, by implication, that he is challenging the reader to a new way of thinking.

In a parenthetical way, Melville tells us that the "Etymology" is "supplied by a late consumptive usher to a grammar school." What is an usher, and why would Melville resort to such an image? The term *usher* ultimately is related to the Latin *os*, which means mouth or orifice. An usher, therefore, is one who has the duty of making introductions orally between unacquainted persons. An old British use of the term refers to an assistant teacher in a school. From these observations, it is clear that Melville means to introduce us to an "unknown" kind of story, one with which we are unacquainted. An usher is not a forceful sort of figure, being of less "rank" than those whom he introduces. Once the introductions are complete, he can easily be ignored—as indeed is the case in our novel. The depth of the conversation between the text and reader that follows the introduction depends solely upon the quality of the parties involved. In this sense, what follows is as fragile as it is profound.

Melville relates that the pale usher (he shares his whiteness with the whale) was "ever dusting his old lexicons and grammars," an activity that "somehow mildly reminded him of his mortality." It is not the grammars that remind him of his mortality; it is the *dusting* of them. Why should this be the case? It is true that Genesis 3:19 teaches that man is dust and shall return to dust at death. But more than this, the dust that accumulates on man-made objects symbolizes their deterioration at the hands of time, that is, their finitude. Just as books must be continually dusted through the passage of time, so must words and concepts. This is what etymological study does. The dusting of "old lexicons and grammars" means getting at long-forgotten and deeper layers of the meaning of language itself.

This insight is the basis of Melville's theology. Ishmael's yearning for the sea reflects his search for a "dust-free" zone. Unlike the usher, he is dissatisfied dusting with the "queer handkerchief, mockingly embellished with all the gay flags of all the known nations of the world." Ishmael (like Melville himself) must actually set sail for foreign places. Actually, this "late consumptive usher" serves as a kind of opposite to Ishmael, even though he appears only in these few introductory lines. He falls victim to the consumptive death that overtakes the majority of landbound mortals, as they fight mainly against advancing time. Ishmael refuses to settle for such a slow, shallow death. His longing for the sea is a longing for the direct experience of nations (and whales). The enemy on the sea is not dust; it is the more immediate encounter with reality itself. This demand for immediacy is the hallmark of Melville's theology, just as it is of Job's. It is the basic connection point between the two works.

The "Etymology" begins with a quotation from Richard Hakluyt.

> While you take in hand to school others, and to teach them by what name a whale-fish is to be called in our tongue, leaving out, through ignorance, the letter H which almost alone maketh up the signification of the word, you deliver that which is not true.

The silent "h" in "whale" symbolizes the silent aspect of language itself. If this silent aspect is omitted from consideration, then we "deliver that which is not true." Similarly, there is a silent side to the novel itself. And if we do not understand this, then we deliver "that which is not true." Strictly speaking, it is not true, as one often hears, that the story can be read on different levels—adventure story, work of art, philosophical novel, and the like. The silent, hidden side of the story *demands* consideration, or else one falls victim to an untrue reading. In like fashion, Melville's theological reflections penetrate beyond the level of explicit experience and ecclesiastical dogmatism. To fail to take this silent side into account is not simply to hold to a childish and immature faith; it is to be wrong. Indeed, for Melville, it is the theological task of his writing to jolt the immature and dogmatic perspective toward an understanding of the implicit way that God deals with the world. He takes the literary license of mixing falsehood with truth in order to clear the way for deeper insight—a point that Melville makes in the partly fictional listing of foreign words for whale immediately following the quotation from Hakluyt.

Melville reinforces the point that this is to be a novel about language in the "Extract" preceding chapter 1. He parenthetically notes that the "Extracts" are provided by a "sub-sub-librarian." What is a "sub-librarian"? The term must refer to someone who penetrates literature's "depths," someone who does not operate on the surface level of meaning. This librarian exists not simply in a "sub" region, but a "sub-sub" region, thereby intensifying the ambiguous meaning of things beneath the surface. The life and work space of this dreary soul is described in the introductory sentence in these terms:

> . . . this mere painstaking burrower and grub-worm of a poor devil of a Sub-Sub appears to have gone through the long Vaticans and street-stalls of the earth, picking up whatever random allusions to whales he could anyways find in any book whatsoever, sacred or profane.

Like the Sub-Sub, Melville himself will lead the reader through the long Vaticans (ecclesiastical theology) and street-stalls of the earth (where Moby-Dick himself lives). Neither is adequate unto itself. It is the "street-stalls of the earth" that reveal the silent, hidden side of theology.

"Extracts" proper begins with five Old Testament quotations, which theologically anchor the story that is to follow. The first is from Genesis 1:21: "And God created great whales." This text is fundamental, for it establishes the moral complexity of the universe that the whale symbolizes for Melville. Although not quoted by Melville, Genesis 1:21 concludes after recounting the creation of watery creatures and winged fowl that "God saw that it was good." Melville's omission of this statement places the whale above simplistic moral categories. The important thing is that the whale is from God; whether it is evil or good in human eyes, even if it be good in God's eyes, is a hermeneutical problem to be encountered variously by different readers of the text. Of primary significance is the establishment of the story in a realm beyond good and evil, the realm of God. The remaining Old Testament references establish basic features of the ensuing story. For example, the first of these establishes the close connection between the inner meaning of the novel and the Book of Job.

> Leviathan maketh a path to shine after him;
> One would think the deep to be hoary (Job 41:32).

I will begin my discussion of the Book of Job by following this thread of thought that leads from the hoary deep of Moby-Dick to the hoary stature of Job himself.

The promise and limits of American typology. Moby-Dick reveals the new American type that emerged in the period of the American Renaissance. Melville's new man who embodies the American mythos no longer displays the confident identity of the earlier, simplistic models of Jefferson and Franklin. With that loss of innocence, American theology is truly born. In fact, it would not be an exaggeration to say that American theology begins with the three opening words of chapter 1: "Call me Ishmael." From this point onward, the figure of Ishmael replaces Franklin's persona in the *Autobiography* as the central type of the American self. By posing Ishmael as the new American, it is not surprising that Franklin's literary success stands in marked contrast to Melville's failure. However, Melville did not stand completely alone in the new American wilderness. *Moby-Dick* itself is dedicated to a fellow visionary—Nathaniel Hawthorne. Hawthorne's great psychological study of the Puritan pastor Arthur Dimmesdale mirrors the loss of confidence in the New Adam myth that the Ishmaelite type implies. Yet the complexity is greater in Melville's work, and for that reason he stands as a greater theological resource.

What is the theological meaning of Ishmael? First, Ishmael is not the real name of the man who is to function as the narrator. We only know him by his *typological* name, not by his real name. Only if his identity is forced on us in this way can the old, naive typology be overthrown. Since he appears to us in a distorted way, we might well imagine that this occlusion characterizes the entire book. A distinguishing feature of the new American type is the distortion that surrounds him, in contrast to the previous type, who was marked by supposed clarity of vision. However, the significant theological meaning of this Ishmaelite figure is contained in the way that it expands on the basic American mythos. This expansion draws deeply from the biblical Ishmael, even as it alters and amplifies this source. The name Ishmael appears initially in the Genesis account in a word from the angel of Yahweh.

> Now you have conceived, and you will bear a son, and you shall name him *Ishmael*, for *Yahweh has heard* your cries of distress.
> A wild ass of a man he will be, against every man, and every man against him, setting himself to defy all his brothers. (Gen. 16:11-12).

The name means "May God hear" or "God has heard," and stems from Abraham's special petition for a child due to Sarai's barrenness. Ishmael's own existence is problematic due to his birth from the womb of Hagar (Abraham's Egyptian maid-servant) rather than Sarai. His descendants are the nomadic desert Arabs who go their own way and spurn permanent residence and the settled customs of their neighbors. From the standpoint of the conventions of Melville's society, Ishmael was obviously viewed as an illegitimate child. Ishmael is born as a result of the cries of his father, and he wails because of his isolation after birth (Gen. 17-21).

The new American Ishmaelite who is born in this passage embodies characteristics similar to the biblical one. First and foremost, the concept of exceptionality is maintained, only crucially now without the sense of mission. Ishmael is exceptional in that his birth occurs because Yahweh has heard Abraham's cries of distress. Abraham's unhappiness arises from being childless and having no heirs. This situation is in violation of the compact with Abraham (Gen. 12:1-3). Of course, Ishmael is not the heir to Abraham that the original plan provided (Gen. 15:4), a situation that is rectified in the biblical account with the birth of Isaac (promised in Gen. 15 and 17). It is Isaac who will carry on the sense of mission: "With him [Isaac] I will establish my covenant, a covenant in perpetuity, to be his God and the God of his descendants after him" (Gen. 17:19).

Ishmael is the son of Abraham, but he is not his heir. He will be exceptionally blessed as Abraham's son (Gen. 17:20), but he is not called upon for a special mission in the world. As Abraham's son, he receives the benefits of the first part of the call of Abraham: "I will make you a great nation" (Gen. 12:2a). This is more explicit in Genesis 21:18b: "I will make him into a great nation." However, this greatness will have the loss of the sense of mission that is contained in the original covenant. It is precisely the ambiguity of Ishmael's relationship to the Abrahamic covenant that informs *Moby-Dick*. Melville wrestles with this ambiguity from the opening three lines of the novel. It is the primary theological category by which Melville struggles with the question of religious meaning: It is, in Gadamer's terms, the essential American prejudice that remains operative into our own day.

Ishmael is the one whom God hears. He is born in distress and he remains in distress throughout his life. The sounds that God hears are the sounds of protesting, weeping, and wailing. In this way, the corpus of *Moby-Dick* represents Melville's protest against his destiny in being the Ishmaelite son of the Abrahamic covenant—that is, not merely a man who has no mission among the nations, but a man who missed this greatness only because of the fateful circumstances of his birth. For Ishmael, the loss of the covenant ensued from having an Egyptian mother who stood outside the covenant. For Melville, life in God's New Israel had likewise become slavery in Egypt because the culture that had nurtured him also stood outside the covenant. One is reminded here of Chesterton's description of America as "God's almost chosen people." It is the sense of chosenness, without the sense of mission, that established the ground of American theology. It is the reason why the American experience is inherently theological (and not philosophical or aesthetic), and why the Bible (especially the Old Testament) remains the fundamental interpretive document of the American experience and the resource to which America must always return to reimagine herself.

It is the task of American theology to interpret ever anew this sense of chosenness and blessedness, along with acknowledging the loss of mission that accompanies America's experiment. Since Melville, it has become centrally important for the theologian to inquire as to the specific content of America's sense of chosenness and blessing. This is the positive, constructive force of American theology. But the negative, prophetic component is equally crucial. For the great danger is that America will assume by force the sense of mission that narrowly escapes her. This is precisely the perversion that the maniacal Ahab embodies. It is Melville's prophetic message to his fellow Americans that Ahab's destiny will be their own, unless they relinquish their sense of mission. The theological understanding of technology in America begins when it imitates the will of Ahab, serving as a tool for the forced implementation of the lost sense of mission. In this way Melville reminds us that technology is not ethically or theologically neutral in America, but a central matter for religious consideration.

Amidst the plethora of biblical types, images, and allusions that occur in *Moby-Dick*, the literary device that programmatically establishes the central meaning of the story is Father Mapple's sermon on the Book of Jonah in chapter 9 ("The Sermon"). Reinforcing the idea that the novel is about language, it is Melville's most explicitly theological statement and stands as the centerpiece of this primary document of American religious thought. It is all the more important because it affords the Ishmaelite Melville the opportunity to speak as an ecclesiastical "insider." Father Mapple's sermon is pure, unadulterated American exegesis of the Bible. In a sense the whaling story that follows is little more than commentary on this sermon.

Melville's casting of his work as literary exegesis of Scripture could hardly have been accomplished more unambiguously. However, as interesting as a detailed examination of Melville's exegetical method might be (that is, a description of how he changes the wording and meaning of the Book of Jonah by omissions and additions), a theological perspective that has previously eluded literary interpreters is more insightful for our purposes. Close examination reveals that Melville gives his *own* "inside exegesis" of Father Mapple's sermon, as well as the Book of Jonah, in a hidden way in the succeeding chapter (10) entitled "A Bosom Friend." Chapter 10 relates to chapter 9 as the silent "h" to the word "whale" in that it "almost alone maketh up the signification" of the entire work. Whereas Father Mapple's sermon addresses the general problem of human pride, chapter 10 tells us what this pride means in the context of American religious experience. Taken together, chapters 9 and 10 of *Moby-Dick* represent the high watermark of the theology of Ishmaelite typology and constitute a fundamental perspective out of which an American reading of the Bible might take place.

In the beginning of his sermon, Father Mapple states that the Book of Jonah teaches a twofold lesson. This lesson is directed "to us all as sinful men, and a lesson to me as a pilot of the living God" (72). In other words, one aspect is directed to all men, while a second is directed "still more" (79) to God's chosen one, who has an exceptional task to perform. This dynamic, which Melville establishes at this central place in the book, is a further development of the features of his theology already present in his use of the Ishmaelite typology. As a guide for the story that follows, Father Mapple's sermon is also a look backward to the old American Abrahamic theology and a ready explanation as to why it failed. Concerning the part of the lesson that is directed to all men (Americans included), he says,

> But all the things that God would have us do are hard for us to do—remember that—and hence, he oftener commands us than endeavors to persuade. And if we obey God, we must disobey ourselves; and it is in this disobeying ourselves, wherein the hardness of obeying God consists (72).

This general prescription fits all human creatures; it is the root theological problem of human existence. All other problems flow from it, in particular those Melvillian problems associated with democratic values and aspirations, reasoned control of individual emotions, and fanciful flights from the deeper truths of life to which nearly all people fall victim. The failure of the Abrahamic myth itself is anchored in this general human problem.

Much later in Father Mapple's sermon, Melville addresses the problem of chosenness. He begins: "Shipmates, God has laid but one hand upon you; both his hands press upon me. I have read ye by what murky light may be mine the lesson that Jonah teaches to all sinners; and therefore to ye, and still more to me, *for I am a greater sinner than ye*" (78-79). Mapple's lot as a chosen one of God simply carries with it an *intensification* of what is *generally* true for all people. It is now that the awful truth becomes manifest. To be the "anointed pilot-prophet" of God, such as Jonah is, means "to preach the truth to the face of Falsehood." That is the mission of the Abrahamic covenant. That is the ingredient by which all the nations of the earth might be blessed. But it is the aspect of the covenant that eluded the Abrahamic typology and reduced it to the Ishmaelite typology; that is, exceptionality without mission. Like Jonah and Ahab, America had fled from her original covenant because of her inability to disobey herself and follow God. With that flight the peculiar problems of American religious thought began in all gravity. Father Mapple begins the conclusion to his sermon with a series of woes. Embedded in this series are two statements of particular interest that act as a bridge to Melville's extraecclesiastical theology that unfolds in the subsequent chapter.

> Woe to him who, in this world, courts not dishonor! Woe to him who would not be true, even though to be false were salvation (80).

For Melville, to pursue "Gospel duty" is to court dishonor and to be true. He finishes: "Yea, woe to him who, as the great Pilot Paul has it, while preaching to others is himself a castaway!" In the novel Captain Ahab is the "castaway." Ahab's "preaching" is nowhere more explicit than in chapter 36, "The Quarter-Deck," a sermon that exhibits some structural parallels with Father Mapple's. As we know, King Ahab in the Old Testament was "worse than all his predecessors" (1 Kg. 16:30). Among other crimes against Yahweh, he constructed "a sacred pole" used in the worship of Baal (1 Kg. 16:33), analogous to the harpooners' poles utilized by the crew of the *Pequod* in the hunting of Moby-Dick. As a "castaway," Ahab fulfills the definition of "a shipwrecked person," or "a discarded or rejected person or thing." Like the Old Testament Ahab, he has turned his back on the old Abrahamic faith. In the vision of Micaiah, the death of Ahab has the following result: "I have seen all Israel scattered on the mountains like sheep without a shepherd. . . ." Like King Ahab, the death of Captain Ahab is meant to be understood in intimate relationship with his people. As the personification of the lost covenant, the American experiment itself is shipwrecked and rejected. Only Ishmael, who alone survives the shipwreck of the *Pequod*, offers a glimmer of hope. He still retains the blessing of God, even if the religious mission of the covenant is only a mirage. So which will America choose, Ishmael or Ahab? The types of Adam or Abraham are no longer accessible. Obviously, Melville would have the reader choose Ishmael.

Melville points us toward the way of redemption in the chapter following Father Mapple's sermon, entitled "A Bosom Friend." It is the chapter that gives fullest expression to his gospel of salvation for the American religious experience. It is built on the nonsectarian premises of Franklin's and Jefferson's expansion of the new American Abrahamic type. The chapter records Ishmael's encounter with the religion of "the dark complexioned," "head peddling" harpooner Queequeg. Melville describes Queequeg as "George Washington cannibalistically developed." Just as George Washington was looked upon as a type of the Old Testament Moses, who led his countrymen out of the wilderness as the father of his country, so too does Ishmael's relationship with Queequeg offer some hope of leading America out of the new wilderness. The fact that Ishmael is saved from the eventual shipwreck of the *Pequod* by Queequeg's floating coffin stands as a prophetic warning about ignoring Melville's message.

Chapter 10 recounts how Ishmael, returning from Mapple's sermon, encounters Queequeg in their joint room at the Spouter-Inn whittling a little "negro idol." While closely watching this strange activity and contemplating the extreme serenity of this man 20,000 miles from home, Ishmael experiences a melting of the "damp, drizzly November in my soul" (23) that had motivated his return to the sea. "No more my splintered heart and maddened hand were turned against the wolfish world. This soothing savage had redeemed it" (83). He continues with the caustic comment, "I'll try a pagan friend, thought I, since Christian kindness has proved but hollow courtesy" (84). "Christian kindness" refers, of course, to those "Christians" whom Ishmael has normally encountered, not the Christianity of Father Mapple. Indeed, Ishmael's fully developed theological statement, which follows directly, explains the inner meaning of the second aspect of Mapple's sermon.

> I was a good Christian; born and bred in the bosom of the infallible Presbyterian Church. How then could I unite with this wild idolator in worshipping his piece of wood? But what is worship? thought I. Do you suppose now, Ishmael, that the magnanimous God of heaven and earth—pagans and all included—can possibly be jealous of an insignificant bit of black wood? Impossible! But what is worship?—to do the will of God—that is worship. And what is the will of God?—to do to my fellow man what I would have my fellow man do to me—that is the will of God. Now, Queequeg is my fellow man. And what do I wish that this Queequeg would do to me? Why, unite with me in my particular Presbyterian form of worship. Consequently, I must then unite with him in his; ergo, I must turn idolator.

"I must turn idolator." This brief statement is the apex of Melville's theology. It is the unfolding of Mapple's concluding woes outside of the ecclesiastical setting.

> Woe to him who, in this world, courts not dishonor! Woe to him who would not be true, even though to be false were salvation.

To court dishonor, to be true, means to turn idolator. Impossible as it might seem to orthodox doctrine, Melville believed that this turn to "idolatry" was essential in America in order to do the will of God.

If one views that covenant from this perspective, things appear in a new light. Genesis 12:36 reads: "All the tribes of the earth shall bless themselves by you." Melville perceives that the tragedy of the American religious experience is that this call of Abraham (and his sons) has been misread by succeeding generations of Americans as a commission to witness for God and to *impose* the biblical faith upon the pagans. The oppressive figure of Captain Ahab is the ultimate symbol of this tendency: a man who must fight directly against the elements themselves, which he perceives to have rebelled against him. Ahab is the logical extension of Hawthorne's Puritan pastor Dimmesdale, several generations removed and set in the midst of the secular world. This too explains the existential ground (the first point of Mapple's sermon) upon which the peculiar American problem is defined, namely, the problem of disobeying ourselves and obeying God. The most difficult part of the Abrahamic covenant is the disobeying of ourselves upon the reception of the blessing of God. It was the challenge that the American religious experience had utterly failed to achieve. Ishmael, who still reaped the benefits of the blessing to Abraham, only senses the meaning of the mission in relationship with Queequeg (in Melville's language, they become a "married pair"). Queequeg himself, several chapters later, makes the summary statement: "We cannibals must help these Christians" (96). For Ishmael's part, the salvation that Queequeg has brought him means that "I clove to Queequeg like a barnacle; yea, till poor Queequeg took his last long dive." Though Ishmael has met his salvific Christ, he must still confront the alter ego of the American self in the person of Ahab.

The world as canon beneath the canon. Queequeg, the "primitive" man of nature, leaves the church service during Father Mapple's sermon and returns to carving idols. The sermon is intended only for white Christian America, and is meaningless for someone of Queequeg's history. In chapter 12, the narrator notes, "But, alas! the practices of whitemen soon convinced him [Queequeg] that even Christians could be both miserable and wicked; *infinitely more so, than all his father's heathens. . . .* Thought he, it's a wicked world in all meridians; I'll die a pagan" (italics added). Further on, we learn that Queequeg was the son of a king and heir apparent to his tribal throne. However, because of his sojourn in the West, he was fearful Christianity, or rather Christians, had unfitted him for ascending the pure and undefiled throne of thirty pagan Kings before him. But by and by, he said, he would return,—as soon as he felt himself baptized again. For the nonce, however, he proposed to sail about, and sow his wild oats in all four oceans. They had made a *harpooneer* of him, and *that barbed iron was in lieu of a sceptre now* (90, italics added).

For Melville, much of the paganism that Christianity wished to supplant was superior to it. The "Christian" West was really interested in technology rather than religion.

The black "savage" and the white Christian Starbuck represent the pivotal figures in Melville's theological treatment of the American self. Queequeg embodies precisely those attributes that are tragically missing in the one-legged, "demasted" Ahab who undertakes mad flight from the inner theological meaning of the American myth. Queequeg practiced in his life precisely the theological principle that Mapple had advocated to his congregation, namely to court dishonor in order to be true. What better way to describe Queequeg's experience in the Christian West. Moreover, Queequeg's masterful ability with the white man's harpoon amounts to little less than idolatry. Ishmael's theological insight in the Spouter-Inn—"I must turn idolator"—arises because that is precisely what Queequeg has done in his absorption of Western ways. Against this idolatry, Queequeg in life vainly awaits a new baptism, and perhaps only finds it symbolically in his death at sea.

It is clear that Queequeg is a man for others, even if only Ishmael—of all the characters—comes to this insight. It is quite possible and proper that Ahab himself sees something of this in his summary statement of the man: "Oh, devilish tantalization of the gods" (612). However, the character of Ahab has developed too deeply; he cannot be reached. His earlier self-analysis is only too correct: "They think me mad—Starbuck does; but I'm demoniac, I am madness maddened" (226). Queequeg's coffin can only be utilized as a life buoy for Ishmael *after* the *Pequod* has sunk. Like the New Testament Christ, the significance of his life must be interpreted through his death.

Starbuck, the chief mate of the *Pequod*, is the most religious man—in the Western sense—on board ship. He is a Quaker (157), who is "uncommonly conscientious for a seaman, and endued with a deep natural reverence" (158). The key to Starbuck's religion is in his low murmur as he gazes down at the sea: "Loveliness, unfathomable, as ever lover saw in his young bride's eye!—Tell me not of thy teeth-tiered sharks, and thy kidnapping cannibal ways. Let faith oust fact; let fancy oust memory; I look deep down and do believe" (624). In Ahab's speech before the crew in which he reveals his deadly purpose of hunting Moby-Dick, Starbuck alone opposes him by uncovering the motivation of vengeance. He then exclaims: "Vengeance on a dumb brute . . . that simply smote thee from blindest instinct! Madness! To be enraged with a dumb thing, Captain Ahab, seems blasphemous" (220). But such common sense makes no progress with Ahab, and Starbuck can only murmur: "God keep me!—keep us all!" (222)

The uneasy relationship between the spiritual Starbuck and Ahab reaches a climax in Ahab's cabin (chapter 109), when Ahab confirms his commitment to chasing Moby-Dick, rather than collecting whale oil for the ship's owners. In the midst of this dispute with Starbuck, Ahab exclaims: "There is one God that is Lord over the earth, and one Captain that is lord over the Pequod" (604). Starbuck responds to this blasphemous statement: "Thou has outraged, not insulted me, sir; but for that I ask thee not to beware of Starbuck; thou wouldst but laugh; but let Ahab beware of Ahab; beware of thyself, old man" (605). Ahab's concluding statement, at the time of Starbuck's departure from the cabin, strikes at the heart of Melville's critique of Western religion: "He waxes brave, but nevertheless obeys; most careful bravery that!" (605) Starbuck's carefulness masks his lack of courage in standing up to Ahab. Starbuck has perceived rightly, but he lacks the will to carry out his perception. His failure is the failure of Western Christendom, and reminds the reader of Mapple's sermon: "And if we obey God, we must disobey ourselves, wherein the hardness of obeying God consists." Whereas Queequeg cannot reach Ahab because Ahab can no longer respond to the innocence of natural man—even natural man absorbed into the corruption of Western culture (ch. 132)—Starbuck fails because Christianity has not adequately transformed his natural preoccupation with self-protection. In either case, natural man is powerless in the face of Ahab's madness.

Neither natural man nor nature herself can speak to those forces that drive Ahab. As Starbuck says, Moby-Dick is a dumb brute that smote Ahab from "blindest instinct." For Melville, the whale—any whale—represents "the unspeakable foundations, ribs, and very pelvis of the world" (182). For that reason Melville leaves his chapter (32) on the classification of whales incomplete.

> But I now leave my cetological System standing thus unfinished, even as the great cathedral of Cologne was left, with the crane still standing upon the top of the uncompleted tower. For small erections may be finished by their first architects; grand ones, true ones, ever leave the copestone to posterity. God keep me from ever completing anything.

As a complement to the ambiguity and indifference of the world, Melville follows a literary technique of incompletion. If the world is "incomplete" with regard to man, then we should face up to the full implications in dealing with it. As he writes in another place, "There are some enterprises in which a careful disorderliness is the true method" (465). "A careful disorderliness" can keep our intuitions of truth from becoming dogmatic falsehoods.

At its deepest levels, the technology developing so rapidly in nineteenth-century America was no real escape from the dark side of life. At one point Ahab gazes at his quadrant and exclaims,

> Foolish toy! babies' plaything of haughty Admirals, and Commodores, and Captains; the world brags of thee, of thy cunning and might; but what after all canst thou do, but tell the poor, pitiful point, where thou thyself happenest to be on this wide planet, and the hand that holds thee: no! not one jot more! Thou canst not tell where one drop of water or one grain of sand will be tomorrow noon; and yet with thy impotence thou insultest the sun! Science! Curse thee, thou vain toy; and cursed be all the things that cast man's eyes aloft to that heaven, whose live vividness but scorches him. . . . (633-34).

Even Ahab, bent on the full employment of technology for his vengeful purposes, is capable of a moment's insight into the vanity of technology. His soliloquy represents a perspective at odds with the developing American self. Technology tends to rob us of the questioning stance that we must have toward a world whose foundations lie too far beyond us to understand. Technology provides all too easy answers to our questions about the world, if it does eliminate them altogether. Moreover, it evades the questions with which the universe itself interrogates us when we contemplate it.

Finally, Melville gives us the clearest insight into his view of Christianity, based upon his view of nature, with these words: "Doubts of all things earthly, and intuitions of some things heavenly; this combination makes neither believer nor infidel, but makes a man who regards them both with equal eye" (480). It is the summary statement of Melville's mature religion. It is Father Mapple holding his head in his hands after a sermon in which he has proclaimed: "I am a greater sinner than ye." It is the in-between world of Queequeg and Ishmael. It is the fundamental religious reality at play in the American mythos that Melville was valiantly attempting to reimagine in his time. The utopia of America was ripening into ectopia. The American space—set aside by its early mythmakers—had failed to escape the universal ambiguity of nature. And Melville knew, from his many years on the sea, that when myth and nature do not coincide, it is nature that has the last word. It was only the dreamy-eyed "Platonists" who didn't know that, because they failed to test their mythos against the real world. With this in mind, let us turn to the biblical Job—a man forced into hermeneutical reflection after encountering the harshness of reality.

• The Hermeneutical Job •

The theological grounding. In the Book of Job the central concern is not one of several possible theological issues; it is the man Job himself. This is made clear at the beginning of the book (1:1-5), an introduction that recalls the opening of 1 Samuel, which begins: "There was a man from Ramothathim—Zophim." Job commences more existentially: "*A man* there was in the land of Uz." To Job, unlike Samuel, God appears at the end of his story instead of at the beginning. Job is a man who must stand alone until he hears the voice of God out of a storm, at the end of a long and lonely struggle with himself and with others. Furthermore, we know nothing about the cultural context of Uz. We only know that it is not Israelite. The lack of specific detail about Uz means that we ought to understand it in universal cultural terms that are applicable to all societies. The land of Uz transcends geographical space and time. Job is a mythological figure who is no *one* human being; rather, he represents, to a greater or lesser degree, *every* human being.

I shall continue, briefly, the comparison with Samuel. In many ways one is the mirror image of the other. We can quickly gain a sense of the breadth and depth of ancient Israelite religion in this way. Samuel is the boy who is chosen by Yahweh before he is born. His birth has miraculous overtones. Not only does Samuel *not* seek God at the time when Yahweh calls out to him, he also does not even recognize God's voice. On the other hand, Job is the man who is stricken in the prime of life by events that compel him to seek out the deeper, spiritual meaning of (his) life. Here all the events of the book lead up to the appearance of God in a dramatic theophany. These two biblical figures witness to the richness of the ways that God interacts with human beings. Samuel, who grew up in the presence and service of Yahweh, is a man of Yahweh's own heart, will, and emotion. He is the greatest man in all Israel in his time, and he is remembered as a giant in the faith for all succeeding generations. Job, the individualist, the non-Israelite, shows us the way of the outsider to Yahweh. To a person such as Job, Yahweh comes rarely, and as a judge rather than as a father or a friend. To Samuel, Yahweh need only *show* himself. To Job, who is distant in spite of his religiosity, Yahweh speaks more in the categories of judicial dispute. While both are figures of crisis and transition in ancient Israelite society, we gain the impression that Yahweh accompanies Samuel in each problem that he must face with instructions and guidance. However, to Job, Yahweh only appears once, and then not as a shepherd, but as Prosecutor and Judge.

The overarching impression that one gets of Job from these opening verses is that of a man who was at peace (תָּם), living justly (יָשָׁר); one who found the deepest meaning of his life in his extended family and economic interests. These are the sorts of things that we know about Job, rather than his genealogy, time of life, and place of residence. Was he a religious man? Yes, but what we know of his religion touched only those familial and economic interests. In the opening verses of the book, Job's external religiosity might well be the result of his desire to maintain his social and economic status quo. The adjectives that are used to describe Job (תָּם, יָשָׁר) refer to the external features of his life and encompass the totality of his moral and religious well-being. Job seems, in the context of the religious community in which he participates, an ideal product. What, of course, remains to be tested is the inner life of such a man. What still must be considered is the question of whether the inner life corresponds to the outer life. That these cannot be taken as one is part of the meaning of the religious crisis that marked the time this book was composed.

The one who is to probe the interior quality of Job's life is Satan. That he wishes to do that, and has the right and duty to do it, cannot be disputed.[2] Satan comes not so much as an enemy of man or God, but as a breaker of idols. He is the one who demands that the truth shine forth, that all hypocrisy be shown for what it is. Although his power is less than God's, his eye is sharper and he is not so easily deluded by the outward form of things. Perhaps he is not so burdened by the mercy and loving kindness that characterizes the general biblical view of the relationship between Yahweh and the world. This characterization of Satan exhibits no real enemy of human beings, but a figure to be feared nonetheless. It is characteristically human to live in the realm of the external, and to keep the internal realities hidden.

The middle part of the introduction (1:6-2:10) describes the affliction of Job in two very similarly constructed parts (1:6-22, 2:1-10). The similarity between these parts is remarkable (the variations are placed in italics).

---

[2]Friedrich Horst, *Hiob*, Biblischer Kommentar altes Testament, 16:1 (Neukirchen-Vluyn: Neukirchener Verlag, 1968) 13-14.

1:6-12: One day the Sons of God came to attend on Yahweh, and among them was Satan. So Yahweh said to Satan, "Where have you been?" "Around the earth," he answered, "roaming about." So Yahweh asked him, "Did you notice my servant Job? There is no one like him on the earth: a sound and honest man who fears God and shuns evil." *"Yes," Satan said, "but Job is not God-fearing for nothing, is he? Have you not put a wall around him and his house and all his domain? You have blessed all he undertakes, and his flocks throng the countryside. But stretch out your hand and lay a finger on his possessions*: I warrant you, he will curse you to your face." "Very well," Yahweh said to Satan, "all he has is in your power. But keep your hands off his person." So Satan left the presence of Yahweh.

2:1-7: Once again the Sons of God came to attend to Yahweh, and among them was Satan. So Yahweh said to Satan, "Where have you been?" "Around the earth," he answered, "roaming about." So Yahweh asked him, "Did you notice my servant Job? There is no one like him on the earth: a sound and honest man who fears God and shuns evil. *His life continues blameless as ever: in vain you provoked me to ruin him."* "Skin for skin!" Satan replied. *"A man will give away all he has to save his life. But stretch out your hand and lay a finger on his bone and flesh;* I warrant you, he will curse you to your face." "Very well," Yahweh said to Satan, "he is in your power. But spare his life." So Satan left the presence of Yahweh.

The two aspects of the account turn on three axial points, indicating three perspectives that the narrator wishes to provide.

1. Through the dialogue between Satan and Yahweh we learn that the afflictions that Job is to suffer are not the consequences of any actions of his own. His suffering is to have a theological ground, something that originates in the interrelation of the divine and earthly realms.

2. The afflictions of Job are existential, not limited to metaphysical speculation. Job is provoked to think about his lot, and he must consider his received theology in the light of this new experience.

3. Because of Job's refusal to curse God for his affliction, he remains a person of integrity and uprightness. The text could not emphasize this point more stringently. Before the first affliction, Yahweh says: "There is no one like him on the earth: a sound and honest man who fears God and shuns evil." 1:22 concludes the first afflictions with the comment that "in all this misfortune Job com-

mitted no sin nor offered any insult to God." The drama continues in the second round of afflictions, when Yahweh repeats his judgment of Job (2:3). Finally, in spite of the harshness of these difficulties, the text concludes: "And in all this misfortune Job uttered no sinful word" (2:10).

It is possible to misunderstand the central meaning of the book by assuming, for several reasons, that Job did not live up to Yahweh's characterization of him. Why? First, in the evaluation of his three friends, Job was a sinner. Second, this position is strengthened, reinforced, and compounded by Elihu. Third, and most emphatically, the great speeches of Yahweh at the end of the book (38-41) have the tone of an opponent's attack in a court of law. Fourth, Job's final words in the book (42:1-6) retract his previous statements and speculations, and acknowledge that his questioning had gone too far. With the weight of this evidence against him, how can we still maintain Job's innocence? The answer to this question penetrates to the deepest levels of meaning of the book. The answer certainly is not that Job has been sinful in his questioning. No doubt he has been *ignorant* of many of the ways of God and the world. What has made Job different from other human beings ("There is *none* like him on earth," 1:8, 2:3) is that he refuses to live in hypocritical ignorance, once he is made aware of it through the pain (הַכְּאֵב, 2:13) of his existential suffering. The collection of speeches that follow represents Job's struggle against his ignorance (not *sin*!) of the ways of God and the world. Rather than being a denial of his original state of integrity and uprightness (1:1), this struggle is an affirmation of it. In the sense that he will not allow lies to exist, the struggle confirms Job's heroic stature.

At the conclusion of this introductory section, we find a remarkable picture. Job does not, as one might have expected, go to the priest for help in solving the question of his suffering. Remarkably, he does *not* turn to his friends. Rather, his supposed friends come to him, and sit with him in silence for seven days and seven nights. From what follows in the dialogue, we can only conclude that Job did not turn to the friends and the religious community because he entertained little hope of finding an answer to his problem in the traditional theology. The inability of his friends to convince

Job (and ultimately, God!) of their description of his situation represents the failure of this theology. The conflict between Job's denial of theological orthodoxy, and the inability of his friends to grasp the meaning and significance of this denial, stands as the creative thrust of the book.

The promise of Job's hermeneutics. The Book of Job ought not to be generically classified as a dialogue in the usual sense. It is, of course, peculiarly interested in language and speech. In fact, it is a collection of speeches framed by a narrative that defines the boundary of meaning of those speeches. This does not mean, however, that one ought not to think of these speeches as interrelated. On the contrary, the deeper meaning of the book only begins to emerge when we interpret these speeches in their *incongruent* relationship. There are three main divisions of speeches in the book: (1) The three cycles of the friends and Job (3-31); (2) the monologue of Elihu (32-37); and (3) the final two cycles between Yahweh and Job (38-42:6). Because these speeches form the heart of the book, it is particularly instructive to examine them literarily as an initial step, in order to gain a vantage point by which we may interpret the narrative context. This is *not* to be a procedure based on literary theory arguing that the prologue and epilogue (1-2 and 42:7-17) stem from a source other than the speeches (3-42:6), for our interest is strictly the interpretation of the text as it now stands. Rather, one is driven to the speeches as the heart of the book because everything in it is so heavily weighted toward them.

The cycle of speeches between Job and his friends is a dialogue in appearance only, because no real exchange of thoughts takes place. Quite simply, the speeches are monologues in the *style* of dialogues. Such a strange literary device does not reflect a weakness in the literary abilities of the writer, but represents a significant aspect of the overall meaning of the book. The friends are unable to communicate with Job, and he with them, because Job's experiences in the prologue have robbed the two parties of a common ideological foundation. We must imagine that the theological posture of Job before the onslaught of Satan was very much in the same tradition as that of his friends. But Job's withdrawal from the setting of his misfortune in 2:8b (וְהוּא יֹשֵׁב בְּתוֹךְ־הָאֵפֶר) symbolizes the beginning of his withdrawal from this shared world view. The en-

tire corpus of speeches, which begins and ends with Job in "dust"
(הָאֵפֶר—2:8b, 42:6b), represents an incubation period for the emerging theology that is manifest in the final Yahweh speeches. In
the beginning after seven days and nights of silence, Job's opening soliloquy in chapter 3 establishes an existential reality that
remains inaccessible to his friends. If *only* Job at this point had
spoken *against* the causal law of reward and punishment for virtuous and iniquitous acts, then his friends would have had an
opening by which they might argue their case to him. But Job
does *not* curse the shared theology. He does not even curse God.
He curses himself; or more specifically, the day of his birth and
the light of life: יֹאבַד יוֹם אִוָּלֶד בּוֹ (3:3a); לָמָּה יִתֵּן לְעָמֵל אוֹר (3:20a).

Job's repudiation of his very existence is not truly considered by
his friends. They think that his grief has clouded his vision and
caused him to lose sight of the traditional theology. It is just the opposite. His grief has enabled him to see through the traditional theology and the emptiness that it shrouds. From the beginning, and
consistently throughout the speeches, the friends weave an elaborate apologetic for what Job knows is a phantom theology. It is clear
that no dialogue is possible. The friends know that the theology is
logical, valid, and true; and, of course, they are quite right—within
the perimeters of their experience. But Job knows even more profoundly that the theology is a red herring. He cannot engage them
in dialogue because he has experienced what they have not. Furthermore, they did not come to learn from him or to discuss with
him, but to condole with him (לָנוּד־לוֹ) and to console him (וּלְנַחֲמוֹ;
2:11).

From the beginning, therefore, the hoped-for dialogue is a lost
cause. The range of his friends' vision is limited to the pastoral and
they never deviate from this perspective. But Job knows this theology as well as (if not better than) the friends. Their argument
places a just God at the center of human existence and prescribes
an all-inclusive balm of repentance/forgiveness for every human
situation. If Job will only appeal to God in repentance, God will respond. Nowhere in the cycle of speeches does Job propose an alternative theology to that advanced by his friends. He has none to
offer; if he did, then a dialogue in the mode of the Socratic dialogues might take place. Like his friends, Job can conceive of noth-

ing other than a just God who mercifully operates on the schema of repentance/forgiveness. It is in this period of incubation, however, that the genius of Job arises. He seizes upon the friends' exhortations to appeal to God for *forgiveness*, and fashions an appeal to God as a *lawsuit*. The basis of his appeal is his steadfast refusal to acknowledge any guilt. Perhaps his very innocence will suffice to force God back to the center of the traditional theology. Such an appeal is not a new theology, it is a further unfolding of the traditional theology. Job's approach is the stuff of hermeneutics. It is intended to draw out the implications of the "text" (traditional theology). If that theology is a sham, then perhaps God will point in a direction that is more intellectually satisfying. In the encounter his friends draw out more and more of Job's despair as he castigates their pastoral intentions. This despair, in turn, gives birth to the new hermeneutics. Their misreading of Job's situation from the beginning—they mistakenly address him throughout as a sinner—has precluded the possibility of genuine dialogue.

As a result, the relationship of the contending parties progressively deteriorates. Indeed, the deteriorating situation is the key dramatic event of the *three* cycles of speeches. The central topic discussed in the first cycle by the friends is the God-centered repentance/forgiveness theology, succinctly summarized by Eliphaz in 4:17. In response to Job's lament, Eliphaz asks, "Can any man be found just (יִצְדָּק) before his God, or ceremonially clean (יִטְהַר) before his maker?" Yet Job's initial lament did not rest on the assertion of his justness (צְדָק) or cleanliness (טָהַר). Job, without qualification, cursed his existence as a human being *as such*. Eliphaz and his two comrades deduce from this lament the theological judgment that Job *must be* a sinner who has turned from God. This deduction is thoroughly denounced by Job throughout the first cycle in two ways: (1) he castigates the friends in increasingly bitter terms (6:14-30, 7:11-21, and 12:1-17); and (2) he reshapes their insistent call for an *appeal* to God on the basis of the repentance/forgiveness theology (5:8 [Eliphaz], 8:20 [Bildad], and summarily in 11:5-20 [Zophar]) into a heroic call for a lawsuit (רִיב) against God (9:3-35, and summarily in 13:17-28) on the basis of his innocence (13:18a). It is a creative stroke of imaginative hermeneutics. Job ingeniously takes the piety of his friends—grounded in what he alone recognizes to be an inadequate theological tradition—and rereads it in light of his experiences in chapters 1-2. This is a hermeneutic qualitatively different from the analysis of his friends, and the difference is one of the major aspects of the book's message. Their theology is unequivocal; it is a direct imposition of the tradition upon the new human experience. Job's hermeneutic is equivocal; it explores that which the tradition has deemed unthinkable, namely, that a human being could actually contend with God. Of course, such a thing is impossible. It is a sign of Job's desperation and alienation from his friends, from God, and ultimately from himself.

The rapidly deteriorating relationship between the friends and Job accelerates dramatically in the second and third cycles. The hostility that surfaces in the course of the first cycle becomes full-blown in the second. The pretense of friendship comes to an end. They are revealed for what they have really been all along: *judges masquerading as friends* (15:4ff. [Eliphaz], 18:2ff. [Bildad], and 20:2ff. [Zophar]). Their seemingly benign pastoral theology has been a front for an underlying legalism. Job's refusal to submit to their judgments, even though he has no better theology as replacement, has unmasked his friends. This indicates that while from the beginning of the encounter no genuine dialogue takes place, the speeches of the two parties do have a marked effect on one another. The friends are increasingly stripped of all pretense, and the generalities that nurture and feed their theology rise to the surface. Eliphaz characterizes "the wicked" in 15:17-35, Bildad describes the plight of "the wicked" in 18:5-21, and Zophar portrays the suffering of "the wicked" in 20:4-29.

The abbreviated third cycle of speeches (Zophar does not speak) is a fitting capstone to the entire encounter and confirms the dialogical failure. Eliphaz is reduced to a fallacious catalogue of Job's sins (22:2-20), accusations fabricated out of whole cloth, with no basis in fact. The logic of Eliphaz's argument has demanded a guilty Job, and he produces a caricature in his last speech. Bildad, on the other hand, summarizes his position with a pietistical hymn to the glory and dominion of God (25-26:14), apparently in an attempt to prove Job's sinfulness on the basis of God's holiness. Again, the generalities flow. Bildad asserts that *no* man is just (יִצְדַּק)

or morally clean (יִזְכֶּה) in 25:4. Indeed, man is nothing more than a maggot (רִמָּה) and a worm (תּוֹלֵעָה) in 25:6. But by taking such an extreme position, Bildad unwittingly falls victim to the logic of his own generalities. If *all* men can be so characterized, then Job's original complaint in chapter 3 remains unanswered. If man is a worm and a maggot, Job was all the more in the right to curse the day of his birth. Job has never argued that God is *unable* to do what he wills with his creatures, but he questions why God *chose* to cause the suffering that Job has experienced. Bildad's final statement represents the ultimate retreat of the pietistical theologian into the delusions of idealistic platitudes. Job has not defeated him in theological debate. But Job's refusal to engage in dialogue has set the stage on which Bildad might defeat himself. Doesn't it ever occur to him that if *no* man is just or morally clean, then *neither is he?* Apparently not. Such an insight would destroy his theology *from the inside*.

Finally, the omission of a final speech by Zophar needs itself to be interpreted. Rather than taking refuge in lies or an illogical refutation of Job's position, Zophar is reduced to silence. This silence is analogous to Job's silence at the conclusion of chapter 2, in that it signifies an utter breakdown of communication and the elimination of the basis on which dialogue might have taken place. Efforts to reconstruct Zophar's final speech (for example, assigning him 27:13ff.) fail to understand the importance of silence—that it can be just as revealing as speech. In fact, in terms of real communication, silence has characterized the discussions from the beginning. Zophar makes explicit what has been consistently implicit throughout. In place of Zophar's final speech, we find the final great speech of Job in chapters 26-31. This speech is composed of several major parts: the disputation speeches of 26-27, the wisdom hymn in 28, and the great soliloquy of 29-31. The cycle of speeches concludes just as it begins, with a soliloquy by Job. He is alone at the beginning and he is alone at the end. The supposed dialogue has been a farce.

Is it fair to conclude that the encounter with his friends has produced nothing of value? Far from it. Job's refusal to buckle under the pressure of three opponents has helped him wrestle with and clarify his own position. It is true that he has come to no genuinely new theological position in his final statements in 26-31. In many ways, what he says there is only a refined version of what his friends have already said before. He speaks of the greatness of God (26:5-14), the plight of the wicked (27:13-24), and the accessibility of wisdom only through the fear of Yahweh (28). Only in the final soliloquy itself, when he stoutly maintains his innocence (see especially his catalogue of purification oaths in 31), does he differentiate himself significantly from his friends. A potential way out of his dilemma has revealed itself, even it it be a highly problematic one; namely, his hermeneutical appeal to the law as a way of convincing God to displace the emptiness at the center of the traditional theology. That is why his innocence has become such a major issue in his final soliloquy (31). Everything now rides on the validity of this premise. The initial complaint centers on his suffering *as a human being*. After the encounter with his friends, an avenue of hope opens up—perhaps the innocence will be enough to induce God to show the way beyond the traditional theology and to restore meaningful existence. This ploy results from Job's equivocal reading of the traditional theology his friends describe. Their insistence on his wickedness is reshaped by Job into a dogged portrayal of his innocence. Job is not concerned about his justness as a means of favoring himself over his friends (or anyone else). He is interested in his innocence only as a means of convincing God to move to the hollow center of the traditional theology. That is why his entire argument must be interpreted in a hermeneutical sense. The movement of the cycle of speeches between Job and his friends that concludes in 31 has run a full course. What has begun as a personal lament, born in the context of real human suffering, ends in a highly refined hermeneutical expression. That movement gives form and substance to the meaning of the entire book.

The emergence of a theology of world. The speeches of Elihu (32-37) follow on the heels of the traditional theology's breakdown. Job's initial silence marks his distancing from it; Zophar's silence at the conclusion of the third cycle indicates that the theology has spent itself in the course of the encounter: matters stand at an impasse. The dramatic question that remains to be answered is whether or not Job's hermeneutical ploy will work—can the trump card that has emerged in his favor in the encounter with the friends, namely his own innocence, carry the weight that he assigns it? Can it persuade God to move into the void? In short, can he shame God into restoring the integrity of his life?

Elihu's speeches respond with a resounding "No!" to Job's hermeneutical experiment. From the outset his speeches are different in quality from those of his friends. That is why he carefully differentiates himself from them in chapter 32. Unlike the friends, who do not really address Job, but only a caricature of him, Elihu focuses specifically upon the heart of Job's hermeneutics—his appeal to God on the basis of innocence. The question is whether purity and guiltlessness before God is a guarantor of meaningful existence. In a carefully orchestrated attack that is clearly visible in spite of a problematic textual tradition, Elihu challenges the heart of Job's "new hermeneutic." He argues that one man's innocence is of a different quality than God's continual merciful intervention in human affairs. The two parties do not fit on the same scales (33). The ways of God are simply not the ways of men; he is incomparably greater. But God does not use his inherently superior might to overwhelm man and destroy him. Rather, his magnificence is demonstrated in the variety of ways that he utilizes to reach man: to save him from the pit (שַׁחַת) and to enlighten him with the light of the living (33:30).

Elihu contends that since it is unthinkable that God would act wicked or commit iniquity (34:10), obviously Job's suffering must be attributed to something besides God. It is clear that God keeps a strict accounting of worldly matters, only suspending judgment when he wishes to show pity. Would Job really wish to contend with such a one as this? Finally, and most effectively, Elihu argues that it would be a mistake to believe that Job's righteousness has any positive benefit for God (35). God himself is not affected either by man's righteousness or iniquity. This is really the crowning blow to the substance of Job's hermeneutics. At the conclusion of the third speech, Elihu summarizes Job's position as "vanity" (הֶבֶל) and "without knowledge" (בִּבְלִי־דָעַת). Job's hermeneutics is vain and void of knowledge because it is ludicrous to think that a trial with God would solve his problems. The realm of good and evil is a human one, with no effect or meaning in the divine realm. There are no lawsuits in heaven—even if, from an earthly perspective, one *appears* to be in the right. Job's hermeneutical perspective, his exegesis of the tradition, fails to carry its own weight and is doomed to failure.

Elihu's response to Job is much stronger than that of his friends. His friends had responded to Job's plight in life, and had uncritically assumed that God had punished him for his iniquity. Elihu, on the other hand, responds directly to Job's hermeneutics, to his appeal to God on the basis of his innocence. His friends do not alter Job's lamentable position—his life remains meaningless. But the encounter with them does provoke Job's attempt to find a way to the suddenly vanished God. He finds, in his friends' exhortations to appeal to God for forgiveness, a basis on which to declare his new theology, though this mighty effort appears to have been in vain. Elihu conclusively shows that it is unduly presumptuous to imagine that a simple human could contend with God in his omnipotence and wisdom. It is a powerful argument that appears to have no refutation. Job does not even attempt to refute it.

The first of Yahweh's two speeches follows immediately upon the collection of four Elihu speeches. Yahweh appears to Job, after all, in the traditional form of a theophany, not in the context of a trial. Elihu had correctly pointed out the absurdity of such a proposal. However, compelling Yahweh's appearance in *any* format is obviously an achievement of the highest order. The silence and hiddenness of God that stood at the center of the traditional theology, that had defined Job's status up to this point, is now displaced by this theophany. Job's hermeneutic has failed in *substance*, but not in *effect*. And the message that Yahweh leaves with Job is far more revolutionary than commentators usually realize.

Most analysts see little or nothing new in the two Yahweh speeches. After all, Job himself was certainly aware of the majestic, creative acts of God reflected in nature from the beginning (9:3-10). This was certainly a part of the traditional theology that he shared with his friends. In his initial speech, Eliphaz already alludes to this "mighty acts of God in nature" theology. Elihu draws heavily on the same tradition in his hymn to God's greatness in 36:26-37:13. It is certainly true that the beginning of the initial Yahweh speech does little more than restate this "mighty acts" theology with which we are by now familiar. Chapter 38:4-30 is conceived around two aspects of the earth: (1) the "foundations of the earth" (בְּיָסְדִי־אָרֶץ) in verses 4-17—the sea (יָם), the morning (בֹּקֶר), the source of the sea (נִבְכֵי־יָם), and the gates of death (שַׁעֲרֵי־מָוֶת) and (2) the "breadth of the earth" (רַחֲבֵי־אָרֶץ) in verses 18-30—light and darkness (אוֹר/חֹשֶׁךְ), snow, hail, wind, and rain. In 38:31-32, God's power extends over the mythological figures of the constellations.

A new phase of Yahweh's creative wonders begins in 38:33: "Do you know the precepts of the heavens? Have you placed its celestial script on the earth?" What follows is a description of the wisdom (חָכְמָה) structured into the working of the world—especially as that wisdom is visible in *wild* animals, that is, animals that exhibit certain characteristics not introduced by humans. This step the text takes to the natural environment, which has *nothing to do with man*, is crucial for the meaning of the Yahweh speeches. The emphasis here is no longer on the mighty acts of God in nature that overwhelm human comprehension. A subtle shift has taken place. A new kind of magnificence is illustrated in the behavior of wild animals—behavior that is of a different quality than human wisdom. Above all, the way of such beasts is nonutilitarian, or better, nontechnological. This nontechnological, "celestial" script written into the way of the world forms the basis of a new vision for Job. For examples of this nonhuman wisdom, Yahweh points to the lion, raven, wild goat, wild ass, wild ox, [wild ostrich], battle horse, hawk, and eagle. Each beast exhibits its own peculiar "worldly" wisdom, all of which stands apart from human existence. The theological meaning of such wild animals is that a wisdom exists in the world independently from that which is human. The purpose of such beings is to signify to man that *he is not of primary concern to God*. Man is only one aspect of creation and is compelled to view himself as one among many, as one whose wisdom is partial by definition and who *must*, therefore, learn to live within the contours of the community of created things and kings. The purpose of the theophany, then, is to substantiate this worldly "canon" that exists beneath or prior to the traditional theology. We can only know such things if God reveals them to us, because by definition such knowledge lies hidden from us.

The second speech of Yahweh establishes the basic features of this revelation still more profoundly. Following Tur-Sinai,[3] I interpret the entire passage of 40:15-41:25 as referring to one mythological beast, Leviathan (understanding the "Behemoth" of verse 15 as the plural of the common noun בְּהֵמָה, meaning "beast, cattle"). In this reading, the description of Leviathan begins in verse 16, although his name first appears in verse 25. Like the animals that exist upon the earth, Leviathan (and Behemoth, if one chooses the traditional reading) was created along with man ("with you," עִמָּךְ, 15b). Indeed, he was the "first of the ways of God" (רֵאשִׁית דַּרְכֵי־אֵל, 19a). The legend of Leviathan, which has its roots in Ugaritic and Accadian mythology, is that he was the prince of the sea and of wisdom. He was "at first God's weapon-bearer and entertainer, until he rebelled and fought against him and was vanquished by him."[4] The case of Leviathan is mentioned by Yahweh because he is a primordial example of one of God's creatures attempting to contend (in this case as a warrior rather than a lawyer) with him and failing (41:1). This example of Leviathan was of far deeper cosmic significance than is the present case of Job, due to Leviathan's natural superiority in strength and proximity to God. Granted the mythological character of the beast, Leviathan symbolizes a part of creation that exists *independently* of man (cf. 40:25-32). The beast (or "beasts," if one chooses to retain the traditional Behemoth figure of 40:15ff.) represents the deepest structures of created reality. It is of greatest significance that rebellion against God exists at this deepest level of reality, as well as on the surface of human existence. Job's rebellion, to the degree that it exists in his hermeneutical ploy, must be understood in contrast to this larger revolt.

An especially important aspect of human rebellion is the possibility of turning back to God through language—an inaccessible means for the mythological beast. In this regard, man is more "powerful" than the beast. This is, of course, what Job does in his dialogue with the Yahweh speeches (finally we have genuine dia-

---

[3]N. H. Tur Sinai, *The Book of Job: A New Commentary* (Jerusalem: Siran, 1967) 556-59.

[4]Ibid., 561.

logue). In his first response, in 40:4, Job says: "My hand I place to my mouth" (יָדִי שַׂמְתִּי לְמוֹ־פִי). In his second he confesses: "I have spoken about that which I do not know" (נִפְלָאוֹת מִמֶּנִּי וְלֹא אֵדָע, 42:3c). Job realizes from the theophany that God has a purpose or plan (מְזִמָּה, 42:2) in the universe that transcends human understanding. It is in this context that his words (his hermeneutics) are rebellious. It is important to understand that Job repents of this hermeneutics; that is, of his attempt at a lawsuit against God based on his innocence. He does not repent of his *claim* of innocence. Indeed, Yahweh does not require this. In fact, we have every reason to believe that Yahweh was correct in his original assessment of Job in the prologue, namely that he was "perfect" (תָּם), "upright" (יָשָׁר), and "fearing God" (יְרֵא אֱלֹהִים). It is Job's upright character that enabled him to see through the traditional theology. It provided, as well, the creative impetus by which his new hermeneutic might be fashioned—an endeavor that is successful in that it brings about the theophany of Yahweh, but it fails in theological profundity. I can only surmise that Yahweh would *not* have appeared to anyone of lesser stature. Finally, Job's innocence is a strand that is woven throughout the book. Both his silence at the conclusion of the prologue and the theophany are a result of his own inherent knowledge of his righteousness. He does not persist when he realizes that persistence is, in effect, rebellion against God. The theology of human limitation that emerges from the Yahweh speech could be accepted with unanimity by such a man.

Yahweh's speech really is an answer to the complex problem raised by the Book of Job. The heart of that problem is the inadequacy of the traditional theology, which is based on a causal relationship between reward or punishment and virtuous or sinful behavior. Such analytical schemes break down in human existence because man is not the center of the created order. Rather, he is only a part of that order and must share the canons of his existence with other aspects of creation that exist totally independent of him. All too frequently, man runs squarely into the path of onrushing reality, and is injured or destroyed in the process. Such events are symbols, not of God's impotency, but of God's purposes for creation that transcend the human creature. Human categories of right and wrong, good and evil, do not apply in such instances. Human theologies that attempt to embrace the whole of created reality are hubristic and rebellious against God. Human activities that attempt to domesticate the totality of nature are similarly hubristic. Today, one thinks particularly of the technological conquest of nature. Such activities become "sinful" when they violate the otherness of nature. When nature is, in this restricted sense, *desacralized*, then it follows that the impact must be highly significant for man's resulting view of himself and of God.

• Toward a New Theology of American Space •

A close examination of the hermeneutical discussion of *Moby-Dick* and Job reveals a theological dimension of considerable force, especially in view of its symmetry with American historical experience. Five major elements constitute this dimension: 1) The experience of displacement (banishment); 2) The emergence of differentiation (subjectivity); 3) The failure of the stratagems of vengeance/innocence (resistance); 4) The emergence of otherness (objectivity); 5) The return to displacement (assertiveness). This theological dimension reflects the particularities of the American setting and evolves toward a paradigm of universal significance for the total expression of American life. This becomes clearer in a more detailed, point-by-point description.

The experience of displacement. The mature theologies operative in both *Moby-Dick* and the Book of Job are initiated with the experience of displacement. This dislocation has two levels of meaning: (a)The particularities of the main characters' individual experiences (Ishmael, Ahab/Job); and (b) the deeper, a priori condition to which this experience points. Both texts begin in the mood of displacement, of living in the place of *ectopia* ("out of place"). This is clearly visible in the statement "*Call* me Ishmael," which is a way of saying that the narrator has been dislocated from the "place" of his given name. Indeed, the entire architectonics of *Moby-Dick* symbolizes a dislocation of the American experience from land to water. By the time Ahab makes his appearance on the sea, he has already progressed far beyond his own experience of dislocation. Ishmael begins his description of Ahab on first sight in these words: "He looked like a man cut away from the stake. . . ." (168) Ahab's isolation from the crew of the *Pequod* symbolizes his interior alienation. In like fashion the prologue of the Book of Job accomplishes the same sense of dislocation. This illustrates, parenthetically, why the prologue is such an integral part of the book and may not be separated from it.

From the standpoint of these texts, the fundamental religious state of mind may be described by words associated with locality, direction, and ultimately space. Human self-consciousness begins in an attitude of transposition: we do not find ourselves where we want to be. This sense of removal establishes the basic perimeters of life. Satisfactorily responding to this disjunction is a prerequisite to (religious) meaning. Martin Heidegger has correctly presented us with a rich lexicon that captures much of the sense of place and/or dislocation of the human predicament, as in *thrownness*, being *"there"* (from which is derived *Dasein*), *falling, downward plunge*, and the like. Heidegger speaks of *Dasein* as *alongside* the world and living *away from itself*.[5] Such concepts with a spatial element have important consequences for theological discourse, in that they denote a shift from absolute, hypostatic categories to the more referential ones of relationship and directionality. Such a shift is crucial for the task of constructing a theological vocabulary appropriate to the American religious experience and the basic premises of its cultural values. Obviously, the traditional religious image of pilgrimage or journey suggests the same sort of vision, yet it remains to be determined the whence and the whither of this travel. Even the very designation *America* denotes locality, whether by that one means a geographical place or a place in the mind. The view of the author of Job is that time itself is bordered by locality and space, and Melville really does not disagree. From a human perspective, time is the medium through which humans respond to their dislocation, either by seeking their rightful place or by fleeing ever more fully— and resignedly—into dislocation. In other words, time itself can symbolize human dislocation. Rightly understood, it leads us in quest of our rightful place in the world. Time is movement toward location and away from dislocation. In this regard the sentence following *Moby-Dick's* opening line, "Call me Ishmael," runs:

Some years ago—*never mind how long precisely*—having little or no

---

[5]Cf. Martin Heidegger, *Being and Time* (New York: Harper and Row, 1962) esp. 172ff.

money in my purse, and nothing particular to interest me on shore,
I thought I would sail about a little and see the watery part of the
world (italics added).

It is the movement from shore to sea that propels the narrative—not
time. Time is but the medium through which Ishmael seeks his
place in the world. We may make the same general statement about
Job's quest for the meaning of his suffering. This is the major theological distinction to be made between the Melville/Job complex and
that of Pirsig/Jesus—an issue I shall consider more fully below.

In contemporary theology, affirmation of displacement is req-
uisite for mature American religious thought. As is true in all
places, America shares the burden of human displacement. Any
theology that does not start at this point stands outside the hermeneutical context these sources have established. It is the task of
theology here to lead in the task of reimagining the place of America once the limitations of displacement have been firmly established. Of course, this place is as much a place of the spirit as it is
a geographical fact. As such, it must set the dislocated American
self in the context of universally dislocated humanity.

The emergence of differentiation. Awareness of dislocation gives
rise to a perception of differentiation, that is, that the self is different from other selves. It is in this sense that subjectivity is born in
the midst of existential suffering. Ishmael and Job are individualists, acutely aware of their alienation from the human crowd. In the
first chapter of *Moby-Dick* ("Loomings"), we see how Ishmael differentiates himself from the Manhattan crowds ("Manhattoes")
who "must get just as nigh the water as they possibly can without
falling in" (24). Ishmael is one who sets sail and does eventually
"fall in." Of course, Ahab has long since felt the pain of his indi-
viduality, appearing from the first not only as isolated from his
crew and severed from the financial aspirations of his ship's em-
ployers, but also neatly hidden from the reader's view until the *Pequod* had sailed several days at sea (ch. 23). Indeed, Ahab is
admirable in the way that he stands up to his own tragic destiny.
He certainly stands nearer the marrow of life than those of the
crowd who never "leave the shore" of life. Likewise Job, in the prologue and effectively throughout the discussion with the three

friends, is a man severed from his fellow humans, including his wife. This realization of isolation and dislocation represents the dawn of self-consciousness. It is an essential part of the process toward theological maturity, for it arises when the usual way of placing oneself in the world breaks down and leaves one alone. In both *Moby-Dick* and Job this is a necessary step in the development of a critical theology.

Individualization means the recognition of place, that is to say, "I" am in a place that is distinguishable from other places. It is the acknowledgment that life means the quest for one's home, which quest must pass through the discipline of subjectivity. At this point in the theological development, experience is divided into four categories: self, humanity, world, and God. We may call this the *regionalization* of experience. It implies that the natural wholeness of life, which existed before the realization of displacement, is lost forever. The process of individualization means banishment from the naive unity of life that the unthinking naturally embrace. Henceforth community must be achieved through individual *choice*, and can only exist in this way as an artificial entity. Before the emergence of regionality, experience has the illusion of unity and of universality. Job's adherence to the religious customs and practices of his environment symbolizes this sort of naive universality. At this point one misreads the particular for the universal. One sees the family, tribe, clan, or even nation as humankind. As the experience of displacement settles in and the individual becomes uneasy, the family emerges as family, tribe as tribe, clan as clan, and nation as nation. In addition, the collision of such regions upon one another—itself a metaphor of the ectopic human condition—generates the birth of the self. This self is historically conditioned by the same forces, but it is a self now burdened with independence and freedom. This represents a level of complexity unknown in Jefferson's and Franklin's early expression of the American mythos.

In terms of the specific American experience, it is at this stage in the theological development that one must recognize the particularities of the culture. Theology must call attention to a false universalization that is not disciplined by particularization. The American experience is not universal; it is regional. It has no mission to "save the world"; and no one culture is paradigmatic for others. It is not the task of one culture to establish the identity of another. The impetus for cultural salvation, if it is to exist at all, must arise from within the individual cultures themselves. Therefore it is the task of theology in America to "demythologize" myths of special mission. But this demythologization must allow for the distinctiveness of America. It needs to bring into view and critically analyze the fundamental values and social reality of America in light of theological traditions. Just as it must deny the ubiquity of America, it must help safeguard the emerging identity of the American self.

The failure of the stratagems of vengeance/innocence. The mature self emerges in the midst of pain and conflict. In many ways the history of the self is the history of its resistance to its own maturation and development. At this stage the self continuously reacts against the forces that previously drove it into being. It recognizes its own existence as a problem, and it develops a rich variety of ways to combat the pain of its newly perceived location. Here the general theological category of "sin" manifests itself. But we need to ask, what does "sin" mean in this newly defined context? We might define it as disobedience, or perhaps rebellion. But such words are only moderately helpful and may obscure the true meaning. If we wish to continue with the theological language of sin, we must understand it as resistance to the consciousness of dislocation. It symbolizes those forces attempting to divert us into the naive unity of the world that was lost with the knowledge of displacement and the emergence of the self. Sin is revulsion against the regionalization of our experience.

Yet it is instructive that neither of our texts—*Moby-Dick* or Job—has as its main object of discourse the problem of sin, per se. In fact, both advise us, implicitly or explicitly, not to reduce religion to the level of simply combating sin. It is simplistic, for example, to call Captain Ahab a sinful man. Again I cite Starbuck's response to Ahab's programmatic sermon to his crew: "Vengeance on a dumb brute . . . that simply smote thee from blindest instinct! Madness! To be enraged with a dumb thing, Captain Ahab, seems blasphemous" (220). Here we are informed that the nature of Ahab's blasphemy is "vengeance on a dumb brute." Sin, as such, simply does not describe such matters. It is not sinful to hunt whales—even particular whales! In the relationship between self and world that the text relentlessly explores, the term *vengeance* alone adequately describes Ahab's response to the otherness of the "dumb brute." The white whale had done nothing but fight for his own life. Before the narrative begins we learn that Ahab had been "demasted" by the whale in a previous encounter. This loss of limb symbolizes Ahab's loss of place, and vengeance is the false strategy he adopts to regain a measure of what is lost. It is a plan conceived in madness and rage, not in evil design. Sin implies some light of deliberation: Ahab's strategy never emerges from the blindness of his passion.

The text of Job is a far different one at this point, but the same general aspects apply nonetheless. Of course, here we are explicitly informed throughout that the problem of sin misses the point. Indeed much of the book is a polemic against such simplistic thinking, personified in the discussions of Job's friends. Still, Job's response to his displacement has greater affinities with Ahab's program of vengeance than might be otherwise decipherable, if we didn't conceive of the texts in hermeneutical dialogue. Job's displacement is, after all, surely as severe as that of Ahab. It must, of course, be granted that Job does not become vengeful. But that may, in part, be because he has no such opportunity. Job's is an unseen "adversary." His contention is not with the newly perceived otherness of the world, but with the otherness of the divine sphere. This problematic does not allow for vengeance by definition. And yet Job will strike back. The only recourse that he finds in this situation is the theology of innocence. He learns, of course, that this theology is ultimately ineffectual. It is just as ineffectual, I might add, as is Ahab's vengeance. Nonetheless, the text itself will not allow us to reduce Job's strategy of innocence to the category of sin.

In *Moby-Dick* and the Book of Job, two basic responses are made to the pain of the emergent subject and its disruptive experience of regionalization. With the severance of the self from the world there is *vengeance*. With the severance of the self from the divine sphere there is *innocence*. These texts deliberately expand the notion of resistance to particularization beyond the simplistic term *sin*. In other words each represents a challenge to the orthodox religious dynamic of sin/repentance/forgiveness. Instead of the reductionistic "sin" categories, these texts bring an awareness of a pluralistic human response to the problem of displacement.

With the primacy of resistance in the theological dynamic being outlined, it is important to underscore the actual disruptive effect of the American experience on traditional theology. Even as it resists maturation of self by clinging to a naive, jingoistic myth of mission, it destroys the narrow band of theological orthodoxy. In America, resistance to maturation takes on a bewildering plurality of forms. The sin/repentance paradigm is only one of many. The categories of vengeance (especially in the technological age) and innocence are equally widespread. Others, such as ignorance, lie before us to be explored from a traditional, Christian perspective. It is here that the work of exploring the depths of American religious thought creatively begins.

The emergence of otherness. The resistance of humans to the emergence of the subject is universal and durable. All particular human pain is rooted in the isolation of the subject and the recognition that the human predicament is one of displacement. Little wonder that most human activity is devoted to obscuring our sense of dislocation and locating a place of comfort, however transitory. In the paradigm I am developing, time itself consists of two parts: (1) internally, in the gradual recognition of the particular nature of any specific place set in the context of human displacement; and (2) externally, in the call of other regions upon any particular region. Theologically, this means that the proper course in facing up to our subjectivity and overcoming our resistance to it is recognition of the value of otherness. This is the course that mature religion bids us take. It is the one that lies on the other side of the profound anger and frustration produced by experiencing displaced subjectivity.

Ishmael states the case very simply: "I must turn idolator." Such a statement should not be understood in terms of the Christian *becoming* the pagan, but rather that the Christian begins the process of *knowing* the pagan. This rigorous assertion stipulates the supreme worth of the other. It carries the latent certitude of having overcome the resistance to regionalization—not by denying it though a naive unity, but by opening an entirely new area of growth through the other. Similarly, Job's lamentations to his friends and metaphorical trial language before God are both pleas for recognition of his otherness. This otherness is finally achieved in relation to Elihu (man) and Yahweh (God). And God himself reveals the otherness of the world in the Yahweh speeches. In both texts genuine spiritual progress has been made toward solving the problems of human existence.

At this level of progression through the theological model, a great advance is made over the emergence of subjectivity and regionality. Early on, the focus of mind is situated on the self. It subsequently shifts to various strategies of resistance. Then when access is made through the resistances, we encounter the emergence of the other. This does not mean, of course, that one ever completely knows the otherness of the various regions. It is to say that one knows that these regions are other. Furthermore, this stage of development means that one has relinquished once and for all the quest for artificial wholeness that marks the strategies of resistance. Hence one recognizes that the only path to human meaning is through embracing particularity, a particularity that remains bound to the discipline of the one among several. The encroachment of one or more of these spheres upon the individual recalls the experience of displacement. Only in maturity can the individual embrace these reminders and still act in affirmation of life.

In terms of American religious thought, we stand now before the problem of cultural expression, as opposed to jingoistic nationalism. An affirmation of culture is the acknowledgment of particularity. However, extreme nationalism is a strategy designed to inhibit the development of the emergent individual. Theology attuned to a cultural setting must promote the interests of the former, while opposing the distortions of the latter. Affirmation of a particular culture in conscious recognition of its boundaries of experience aids the self's understanding of its own otherness. Since the self, on a surface level, is greatly defined by the peculiarities of culture, the recognition of the worth of other cultures helps solidify the satisfactory character of regionality.

The conscious reaffirmation of displacement. The final movement in theological maturity comes, in a sense, full circle to the beginning. While it is true that one is forever starting anew in the experience of life, this point of origin is obviously different after the full unfolding of theological maturity. No human self ever truly finds its

place. It is human destiny to be born in dislocation and to die in dislocation. What matters in life is not that one escapes this primordial
state, but that one reaffirms it in one's own particularity. This is not
an act of passive resignation, but rather of active acceptance. Job ex-
emplifies this posture at the conclusion of his final speech to
Yahweh.

> I knew you then only by hearsay;
> but now, having seen you
> with my own eyes,
> I retract all I have said,
> and in dust and ashes I repent.   (Job 42:5-6)

Such a statement underlines the futility of resistance and stands as
a full acknowledgement of the otherness of God and world. Ahab
never arrives at this position, for he finds no way through his strategy of resistance. It is precisely because of this that Ahab is such a
monumental figure of American letters. He represents in dark in-
tensity the status of American culture as a whole. His death is the
death of America if it fails in its theological quest for maturity.

I conclude that one ends in dislocation, just as one begins. It is
only the development of the self in response to the knowledge of
displacement that makes religion necessary. And religion happens
in various ways, with various tasks to perform along the way, before maturity is reached. In addition, this very same "religion" can
be easily mishandled and misshaped to become part of the obstruc-
tion to maturity, rather than the vehicle. For that reason religion
needs the secular as an ally in the quest for maturity, especially as
it is manifest in art, philosophy, and science. This does not mean
that all art is "Christian," but it does mean that art in dialogue with
religious traditions can perform a liberating function in the context
of hermeneutical dialogue. Melville's art, illustrated in *Moby-Dick*,
is a case in point.

In terms of American identity, the final result of the theological
journey through *Moby-Dick* and Job results in a myth of dislocation.
Here this dislocation is accepted in the maturity of hermeneutical
vision as the ground for further reflection. Such an experience
ought to be liberating, for only now is the American truly opened

to the potential of his or her culture. No longer does one demand of America the restoration of Eden, but acknowledges its place "East of Eden." Such a loss is not to be lamented. The theological task is to reflect on how and in what sense America might still be a place of blessing, even as it loses its innocent early mythos of purity. Nothing greater can be expected of any place.

THE HERMENEUTICS OF TIME

If Jesus or Moses were to appear today, unidentified, with the same message he spoke many years ago, his mental stability would be challenged. This isn't because what Jesus or Moses said was untrue or because modern society is in error but simply because the route they chose to reveal to others has lost relevance and comprehensibility.[1]

• Pirsig's Cycle of Time •

The ghost of western rationality. In its broadest features, Robert Pirsig's 1974 autobiographical novel is a search for a contemporary means to express values common to ancient Greek and Judeo-Christian heritages of Western civilization. It is, in that sense, a hermeneutical text of the highest order. However, it concentrates almost exclusively on the shape of twentieth-century Western secular society, especially as it exists in America, rather than those religious values that undergird it. Indeed, the foundation of the

---

[1]Robert Pirsig, *Zen and the Art of Motorcycle Maintenance* (New York: William Morrow, 1974) 188. Page citations refer to this edition.

problem Pirsig immediately identifies is the emergence of a "valueless rationality" in the West. In response, he sets for himself the task of determining how we got that way philosophically, and what we should do about it. Since he explicitly traces the origin of our abused rationality to its Greek philosophical heritage (Plato and Aristotle) rather than to the Judeo-Christian heritage, his work is only incidentally religious. But that does not mean that its message is without primary theological significance. Pirsig seeks to change the way we think about *everything*, an achievement that obviously must include theology. His target is expressly the present "system of rationality." In sympathy with those who would "change the system," he observes: "The true system, the real system, is our present construction of systematic thought itself, rationality itself. . . ." (102) The author's attempt to explicate the way we view things today (and cover up our religious heritage) is a kind of philosophical autobiography. He sees in his own story a distorted, contemporary incidence of American mythos. And the image of that mythos, unattached or unencumbered by institutional religion, is a highly problematic one.

Pirsig divides his life in the narrative into two parts, separated in time by a mental disorder "cured" by electric shock treatments. In large part, the narrative is written after this "cure," and consists of reflections on his previous life. He names the figure that drove him to a mental breakdown "Phaedrus." For Pirsig now, this Phaedrus of the past is a ghost. This thought buttresses an early dialogue with his friend John and son Chris (whom he is trying to free from the ghost). To John he concludes,

> The world has no existence whatsoever outside the human imagination. It's all a ghost. . . . It's run by ghosts. We see what we see because these ghosts *show* it to us, ghosts of Moses and Christ and the Buddha, and Plato, and Descartes, and Rousseau and Jefferson and Lincoln, on and on and on (42).

This statement refers to the ghost of Western rationality. This ghost has an analogue with the specific ghost of Phaedrus himself. Shortly afterwards, his son renews the discussion of ghosts.

"Did you ever know a ghost?" Chris asks. I am half asleep.
"Chris," I say, "I knew a fellow once who spent all his whole life
doing nothing but hunting for a ghost, and it was just a waste of
time. So go to sleep."
. . . "Did he find him?"
"Yes, he found him, Chris."
. . . "What did he do then?"
"He thrashed him good."
"Then what?"
"Then he became a ghost himself" (43).

In seeking the "ghost" of Western rationality, Pirsig was searching
for the meaning of Western metaphysics itself. Tragically, Phaedrus's successful apprehension of that meaning ultimately brought
about his own mental destruction. For this reason, the immediate
goal of the narrative, the exploration of Phaedrus's earlier quest of
the ghost, is to forever "bury him" (72). Only then can the author
be freed to live beyond the knowledge that Phaedrus found before
he became a ghost. The image that Pirsig uses here is the knife (cf.
79). As a symbol for rationality, the knife is an "intellectual scalpel"
that "cuts up" the way humans conceive things. Carried too far,
this intellectual scalpel can turn into a tool of self-destruction. This
is what happened to Phaedrus, who was a victim of his own perception of reality.

What can be said of the ghost that Phaedrus found, and how is
it intended to help free us from the problematic of American mythos? The breakthrough in Phaedrus's quest for meaning, the one
that allowed him to penetrate beyond the mainstream of rational
thought, was his realization of the limitations of the scientific
method. After an extensive discussion of the method, and lengthy
quotation from Einstein on the types of people who inhabit the
"temple of science," the author presents the self-termed "Parkinson's law." This law states that "the number of rational hypotheses
that can explain any given phenomenon is infinite" (115). This apparently innocent insight actually carried the most radical implications. Phaedrus found that as he tested hypotheses, and *either*
eliminated or confirmed them, their numbers *increased* rather than
decreased. This implied, furthermore, that all hypotheses could

never be tested because they are infinite. If that were true, then science could not be expected to yield us its goal of provable knowledge. In short, for Phaedrus, his version of Parkinson's law was "a catastrophic logical disproof of the general validity of all scientific method" (115). In this way, perception of the limitations of science became Phaedrus's motivation for studying the meaning of Western rationality.

This particular access to the question led Phaedrus to a further consideration of time. Because the history of science illustrated a random and continuously new interpretation of the data of nature, then "scientific truth was not dogma, good for eternity, but a temporal quantitative entity. . . ." (115) A particular hypothesis was now understood to have a lifespan in proportion to the number of hypotheses generated to explain it. Therefore, the "more the hypotheses, the shorter the time span of the truth" (116). Controlled scientific observation revealed the simple fact that "the more you look, the more you see." "Instead of selecting one truth from a multitude, you are *increasing the multitudes*" (116, italics in text). Thus increasing the multitude of possible truths indicated, for Phaedrus, the ultimate impotency of Western science. In addition, because science had become the central focus of Western rationality, the implication of Parkinson's law extended far beyond the realm of the scientific community. Indeed,

> through multiplication upon multiplication of facts, information, theories and hypotheses, it is science itself that is leading *mankind* from single absolute truths to multiple, indeterminate, relative ones. The major producer of the social chaos, the *indeterminacy of thought and values* that rational knowledge is supposed to eliminate, is none other than science itself (116).

In this way, Phaedrus describes his experience of reasoned irrationality. The result of this is "now seen everywhere in the technological world today. Scientifically produced antiscience—chaos" (116-17). This insight into modern technology—especially American technology—requires a somewhat more extensive discussion.

Pirsig views modern American technology as the natural unfolding of Western metaphysical dualism. This dualism is most visible in our culture in the separation of two kinds of human understanding—classical and romantic. Classical understanding signifies rationality, law, masculinity, and the like; romantic understanding is primarily inspirational, imaginative, creative, intuitive, feminine, and the like. Of course, such an artificial separation is itself part of the classical mind, the "knife of rationality." The ways of understanding *are* ultimately inseparable, though the prevailing philosophy has created a world in which they *appear* to be disparate. This separation represents a distortion of the basic underlying unity, or oneness, of reality. The pathological symptoms manifest throughout technological society are simply the external manifestations of this underlying philosophical distortion. These symptoms include a widespread, irrational, antitechnological sentiment; alienation of laborers from their work; monotony and boredom; loss of pride in craftsmanship, and the like. Pirsig summarizes the matter in referring to "that strange separation of what man is from what man does . . . in this twentieth century" (35), which he sees as the fundamental dilemma of our time. At one point in the text, he draws together his thoughts on the matter in this way: Modern technology falsely assumes that there is only one way to do things, whereas there are in truth hundreds; it has lost its primal association with art, thereby producing ugliness rather than beauty; and it has engendered a truly narrow band through which we may apprehend reason, an inadequacy that generates such irrational areas of thought as "occultism, mysticism, drug changes and the like" (171). In all this, it is important to understand that Pirsig is not opposed to technology as such, but only to the form that has emerged in modern America in conjunction with scientifically produced "chaos." In short, American science and technology are tied strictly to *utility*, to "food, clothing, and shelter," with the result that lives are "emotionally hollow, esthetically meaningless, and spiritually empty" (117). For him this situation best describes the "text" of all of us who would seek our ethical and spiritual roots in the modern world. The question is, where do we go from here?

The transcendence of rationality (east and west). The intellectual assault that Phaedrus made on Western rationality resulted in an impasse: science does not yield a way beyond its own limitations. What methodology exists that can adequately deal with the limitations of method itself? In the throes of this dilemma, Phaedrus moves from inherited rationality to authentic thinking, which commences with attention to what he terms "lateral truth"—the kind of truth you see "out of the corner of your eye" (121). The advantage of this approach is apparent: it can project an angle of vision on one's underlying rational assumptions that may reveal otherwise hidden inadequacies and stumbling blocks. The use of the mind in this mode is not so much bound by the discipline of a carefully conceived methodology as it is given to the quest for truth. The journey that Phaedrus undertakes moves him outside the scientific field to the study of philosophy, and it is in this medium that the book makes its greatest contribution.

Phaedrus's philosophical quest progresses from an exposition of the philosophy of Immanuel Kant, to a period of self-imposed exile in India with its lure of wisdom, before returning to America and ultimately a climactic engagement within an academic citadel of Western rationality—the philosophy department of the University of Chicago. Phaedrus's experience in India is especially instructive for understanding the possibilities and limitations of American mythos. In particular, Phaedrus finds that he is unable to resolve his philosophical search there because his questions are Western, and the answers must conform to this experience. But he is successful in his Eastern journey when judged by his intention of discovering lateral, nonscientific truth. He does gain insights there that will help him overcome the barriers of Western rationality.

Phaedrus finds that the cornerstone of Oriental religion is the Sanskrit doctrine of *Tat tvam asi*, "Thou art that" (145). This teaching admits no duality whatsoever. It is a de facto rejection of the dualism of Western rationality wherein subject is separated from object. It explicitly demolishes the modern technological fallacy of separating the worker from his work. And insofar as it achieves this end, it remains an indispensable advance beyond the limitations of the scientific method. Indeed, this insight marks a major shift in his own understanding, one that he is compelled never to relinquish. It is a way out of the dilemma that had driven him to despair, and it allows the next step in his quest to emerge. The question is not whether the Eastern insight was *true*, but whether it is *adequate* for the Western-based problem of rationality. The following narrative and commentary succinctly tell the story.

> . . . one day in the classroom [at Benares Hindu University] the professor of philosophy was blithely expounding on the illusory nature of the world for what seemed the fiftieth time and Phaedrus raised his hand and asked coldly if it was believed that the atomic bombs that had dropped on Hiroshima and Nagasaki were illusory. The professor smiled and said yes. *That was the end of the exchange.*
>
> Within the traditions of Indian philosophy that answer may have been correct, but for Phaedrus and for anyone else who reads newspapers regularly and is concerned with such things as mass destruction of human beings that answer was hopelessly inadequate. He left the classroom, left India and gave up (italics added, 144).

The price Indian thought had paid for the dissolution of the subject-object split was too great, *given the nature of Western values.* It had achieved a form of oneness at the cost of denying the reality of the phenomenological world. This reality could not be forsaken by anyone who maintained the American mythic tradition—whether in the form of its early formulators (Jefferson, Franklin), or its revisers (Melville). It was an inadequate answer to the problem that had initially directed Phaedrus to the study of philosophy. It would have been meaningless for him to deny his own heritage, so as a result he returned to America: at first to abandon his philosophical search, but ultimately to find his way into the university—initially as a teacher, then as a graduate student in philosophy. The resolution of Phaedrus's quest for truth takes place during this time in university settings—a resolution that encompasses his hermeneutical shift to Eastern philosophy, but also transcends it.

Although the early years of Phaedrus's return to America from India are uneventful from the standpoint of his philosophic quest, he does eventually renew it after being again provoked by consideration of the concept of *Quality.* This term innocently turns up as a word in dialogue with a fellow faculty member: "I hope you are teaching Quality to your students" (180). However, he relates what happens next as follows: "Within a matter of a few months, growing so fast you could almost *see* it grow, came an enormous, intricate, highly structured mass of thought, formed as if by magic" (181). This event is structurally pivotal for the novel. It cleaves Pirsig's narrative into two halves, concluding the second of four major divisions. The second half of the story is centered completely around the meaning and origins of this concept of Quality. Quality, properly understood, answers Phaedrus's quest to transcend the dualism of Western metaphysics. The third part of the novel traces how he came to understand the concept in this way, and the final part relates how, at Chicago, he traces back to the foundations of Western philosophy (ancient Greece) our common Western neglect of the term. This second half of the novel is difficult and extremely rich in theoretical terms. It is convenient to center our limited discussion of this vast material around the textual fragment of Phaedrus that the author terms "the most important of all" (251).

> In our highly complex organic state we advanced organisms respond to our environment with an invention of many marvelous analogues. We invent earth and heavens, trees, stones and oceans, gods, music, arts, language, philosophy, engineering, civilization and science. We call these analogues reality. And they *are* reality. We mesmerize our children in the name of truth into knowing that they *are* reality. We throw anyone who does not accept these analogues into an insane asylum. But that which causes us to invent the analogues is Quality. Quality is the continuing stimulus which our environment puts upon us to create the world in which we live. All of it. Every last bit of it (251).

This text forms the core of the book. It incorporates everything of Phaedrus's struggle up to the moment of institutional insight. It determines everything that subsequently takes place in his life, including the mental breakdown, and his ultimate transformation into the author of the book. In fact, the entire book is simply commentary on the insight of this passage.

What does this text mean? Above all, it represents a certain kind of *monism*. The dualism of Western metaphysics, which had led to the alienation of *homo faber*, especially in the modern world's advanced state of development, is superseded by the unity of the a priori reality of Quality. To the extent that this general recourse to monism is made, the influence of the pantheistic *Tat tvam asi* is clearly visible. However, the text reveals a shift that is crucial, and one that allows Phaedrus to remain true to his Western heritage. "Quality," Phaedrus says, "is the continuing stimulus which our environment puts upon us to create the world in which we live." In other words, Quality acts on the mind. It was only through engagement with Quality that thinking could take place. Both *Tat tvam asi* and Western dualism could now be seen accurately, namely as philosophical (classical) systems; or, now viewed more precisely, variant ways of responding to Quality. The classical orientations of *both* East and West were inadequate to Phaedrus's quest for understanding. But the insight into Quality *was* adequate because it stood in an a priori relationship to both of them. In this way, Indian religion had performed the hermeneutical task of helping break through the impasse of Western metaphysics; but it had failed the Western mind when it dissolved the reality of the objective world, and hence removed the stimulus for thinking itself. For Phaedrus, it is crucial to understand the phenomenological world as *real*. The things that we invent with our minds—whether heavens and earth, or music, religion, and science—*are* reality. They are part of the real, objective world. Of course, such things are a different order of reality than the reality of Quality itself. They find their reality in the environment of this a priori Quality. Thus such things are real because they are derived from reality itself.

Therefore, Phaedrus comes to see that the phenomenological world is no deception. It is not an illusion beyond which we must penetrate to that which is real beneath or behind it (as the Indian Brahman). This teaching has obvious strengths over the dualism of the West. It warns us quite correctly, for example, against the futility of demanding absolute objective truth from a rational and scientific approach to the "facts" of nature. It is only the misperceptions of a hubristic rationality that indicate such facts are absolute, born in the frustration of believing that they "ought" to yield a significance beyond themselves. In truth, the universe *is* a gross deception if we think that rational analysis of it will yield the ultimate meaning of life. However, when one shifts to an analogical way of thinking, thereby understanding the facts of the universe as representing something else—namely Quality—then they are no longer deceptions, but significations. They do not mislead us; rather they point out the way. It was because the professor at Benares Hindu University had not understood this crucial difference that Phaedrus's search there came unsatisfactorily to a close. It was in America that realization finally dawned—a well-tempered realization firmly anchored in the conflicts of his native cultural traditions.

The apriority of time. It is inadequate to Pirsig's work to discuss it simply as a book of abstract ideas, because the ideas are carefully woven into the fabric of a story. The manner in which the story unfolds is part and parcel of the book's meaning. The book assumes the form of a philosophic novel, and works to destroy narrow rationality in the process of its own narration. I wish to inquire in more detail how this happens.

Phaedrus had inherited a dualistic metaphysics that had divided his understanding into the categories of romantic and classical. This metaphysics was later superseded by his hard-earned insight into the a priori character of Quality. This was not a denial that these two modes of understanding were in reality separate from one another. It is just that their separation was rooted in a prior unity. This insight helped Phaedrus understand how scientific truth was grounded in time. Early in the story the author quotes a passage from Einstein that gave Phaedrus particular difficulty: "Evolution has shown that *at any given moment* out of all conceivable constructions a single one has always proved itself absolutely superior to the rest" (115, italics added). Phaedrus finally concluded that "scientific truth was not dogma, good for eternity, but a temporal, quantitative entity that could be studied like anything else" (115). Therefore, from this perspective, time itself yielded the insight that science cannot live up to its goal of objectivity, for sooner or later all theories become dated (cf. Kuhn, *The Structure of Scientific Revolutions*). But Phaedrus comes to realize that this reality should not be a cause for despair. Science and technology should not be abandoned simply because they are analogues of Quality. Understood analogously, they may became heuristic tools for leading one to the source of reality, namely Quality itself.

Obviously, Pirsig's text shares with all narratives the explicit structure of time. But here time is handled in a disjunctive way on simultaneous planes of narration. Pirsig's account of his motorcycle journey from Minneapolis to Northern California is the present tense of the story. His reflections on Phaedrus (his "former personality") and Phaedrus's philosophical journey is the past tense of the story. The two accounts, although chronologically disjunctive, are woven together in the closest possible way. Here images in the narration merge with images in the philosophical discussion. In addition, the unresolved attempt to save his son Chris from the ghost of Phaedrus constitutes the future dimension of the narrative. The explicit purpose of the entire trip is to "bury the ghost of Phaedrus." Therefore, unlike the motorcycle images that arose from the 1960s and early 1970s, Phaedrus's trip does not symbolize a running away or rebellion, but a journey of self-discovery. Rebellion is inherently dualistic, involving antagonism between the self and the other. Pirsig's revolution of thought is monistic, and proclaims a way beyond dualism itself.

In addition, the two planes of narration are analogues for the two types of understanding that frame the author's philosophical questioning from the start; that is, the division into romantic and classical types. The motorcycle journey is experiential and inspirational, filled with instantaneous impressions. It is the "here and now" of the book (cf. 248). This symbolizes romantic understanding. The reflections on Phaedrus lavishly incorporated into this narrative are carefully thought out, rational observations concerned with the underlying form in Phaedrus's view of the world. These reflections carry the narrative beyond the "here and now" in that they are both past and timeless. This is the way of classical understanding. These two kinds of understanding are finally merged in Phaedrus's vision of Quality. In the same way, the "burial" of Phaedrus's ghost at the conclusion of the journey signals the merging of Phaedrus and Pirsig. This, in turn, symbolizes the solution to the problem of Western dualism—the merging of romantic and classical understanding.

The conclusion of the book (part 4) primarily narrates Phaedrus's climactic involvement with the concept of Quality at the University of Chicago. Early on, he had gained the impression that the source of the concept was ancient Greece, and at Chicago he was determined to investigate formally the role it had played in Greek thought. And in spite of the thoroughgoing classical mind-set that he found there, he did fulfill his philosophic quest. Quite naturally, once he had gained this understanding, the Ph.D. (and the Western dualism it symbolized) became meaningless. The despair this engendered, in addition to Phaedrus's overly rational (classical) constitution, resulted in his mental undoing and breakdown. It was on the ashes of this experience, aided by the technology of electric shock treatments, that Pirsig as the author of our text was born. Unlike Phaedrus, Pirsig combines the romantic and the classical: witness the book itself. Pirsig is Phaedrus's new life, beginning with the previous experience of Phaedrus already at hand. What was it he saw that allowed him no apparent access to meaningful existence in America?

The answer, surprisingly enough, was again grounded in the perception of time, and in particular involved the ancient Greek philosopher Parmenides. Pirsig saw the philosophies of Plato and Aristotle as built on the thought of Parmenides. In turn, Western metaphysics was constructed on Plato and Aristotle. Therefore, aetiologically, Parmenides was the key. The central concern of Parmenides was time, or better, permanence. Of course, Parmenides must ultimately be interpreted in the context of the general quest of the pre-Socratics for Permanence (in association with, for example, Anaxagoras). That concept was no longer seen as the exclusive domain of the gods, in accordance with the demythologization process that Greek religion had experienced. Pirsig finds that

> Parmenides made it clear for the first time that the Immortal Principle, the One, Truth, God, is separate from appearance and from opinion, and the importance of this separation and its effect upon subsequent history cannot be overstated. It's here that the classical mind, for the first time, took leave of its romantic origins and said, "The Good and the True are not necessarily the same," and goes its separate way. Anaxagoras and Parmenides had a listener named Socrates who carried their ideas into full fruition (372).

Ultimately, therefore, it was the offending tendency of Western thought to isolate the search for truth from that for the good. This had resulted in the modern emergence of value-free rationality (science and technology). How had it happened? Not, to be sure, by design. Certainly the idea of the Good had played a major role in the philosophies of Plato and Aristotle. Indeed, Plato had made Good the highest idea of all. Aristotle created an entire branch of reason around it, namely, ethics. But for Phaedrus these efforts meant the death of the Good (Quality), rather than its liberation. Hence in the interest of preserving Quality and making it *imperishable*, the formative thinkers of Western thought had rationally *encapsulated* it (cf. 378). In the author's words, they had failed to see that "the Good was not a form of reality. It was a reality itself, ever changing, ultimately unknowable in any kind of fixed, rigid way" (379). In this way, time itself reached to the inner workings of reality. Only the ancient Greek Sophists had really understood this. To the degree that modern science and technology denied perishability, that is, *time*, then they denied Quality itself. This denial of Quality led to the meaninglessness of modern life. Phaedrus had found the answer to his puzzle, but it was left for the resurrected author, Pirsig, to live the life that Quality beckoned.

Once the insight into the importance of the concept of time emerges for the reader of the text, one is struck by the subtle allusions to it throughout. The very first line of the novel, "I can see by my watch . . ." (11), is shortly followed by a discussion of the virtues of various types of highways. This results in an order of preference exactly inverted from that of highway departments, which are concerned with speed and efficiency (that is, "good" time). Also very early in the narration, Pirsig compares his ensuing philosophical discussion to the old American tent-show chautauquas that "were pushed aside by faster-paced radio, movies and TV" (15). The references to time continue. In short, Pirsig's book is fundamentally a discourse on time: how we abuse it, deny it, and flee from it into the shallowness of the modern technoscientific world, which encapsulates it rather than deeply experiences it. The images of the way we *devalue* time in North America are everywhere. We have seen it as an obstacle to be overcome, rather than a means to reality itself. This was a failure Oriental religion had never made, and the source of the Western attraction to science and technology. Westerners had frozen Quality in time by the use of rationality ("word traps," 376). The early Greek sense of ἀρετή had been lost. For the

Eastern mind, conversely, *Dharma* (virtue, duty towards oneself) had remained central, and had disparaged the use of naked rationality. The results of the Western disposition are clear.

> We had built empires of scientific capability to manipulate the phenomena of nature into enormous manifestations of his (Western man's) own dreams of power and wealth—but for this he had exchanged an empire of understanding of equal magnitude: an understanding of what it is to be a part of the world, and not an enemy of it (378).

A consideration of time had revealed the shallowness of the American's existence. In attempting to conquer it, he had himself been seduced.

• The Hermeneutical Jesus •

The disjunctive chronology of orthodoxy. The Gospel writers firmly established their ties to the sacred writings of Israel through a specific, rational methodology. This methodology was grounded in history and frequently took the form of a type/antitype relationship. Concerning these established writings, the early church was acutely aware of their pastness, but it also answered the imperative to make them its own in order to flesh out the meaning of Christian existence. It was, indeed, the very particularity—Judaic—of these texts that necessitated a clear methodological approach to them. It was only through a carefully designed hermeneutics that the texts could speak meaningfully to the Gentile church and even accommodate the broader experience of Jesus within the Judaic environment. This "hermeneutical imperative" in the early church resulted in considerable ambiguity with regard to the understanding of the traditional texts. Ultimately, these texts found their place in the faith as the "Old" Testament; yet serious problems remained. A certain dissatisfaction with their ambiguity vis-à-vis the new faith helped create the environment for the writing of the New Testament. In fact, the clarification of the exact status of the Old Testament within the church was one of the major tasks that the New Testament documents were asked to perform. An illustration of how this was done can be seen at once in Mark's Gospel (1:1-3).

Look, I am going to send my messenger before you; he will prepare
your way. A voice cries in the wilderness: Prepare a way for the
Lord, make his paths straight.

This passage establishes the identity of John the Baptist from the
Christian perspective; but, more important, it establishes the fundamental way in which the "Old" Testament would be "Christian-
ized." Indeed, the designation "Old" Testament itself has
typological implications. The Old Testament would establish the
chronological backdrop upon which the theological meaning of the
subsequent Christ event would be constructed. The genealogical
prologue in Matthew accomplishes the same purpose by utilizing
the rhetorical technique of genealogy (Matt. 1:1-17). Matthew
drives home his intention by concluding (1:22-23),

Now all this took place to fulfill the words spoken by the Lord
through the prophet: "The virgin will conceive and give birth to a
son and they will call him Immanuel."

It very quickly becomes evident to the reader that in order to understand Jesus, he must be set in chronological context—that is, in
a past that is fulfilled by unfolding into the present age.

Although the New Testament is independent enough of the traditions of Israel to interpret them according to its own perspectives,
it is crucial to account for why it did not *displace* them. We know that
this was a live option, especially as the faith was interpreted by its
Gnostic wing. Instead, the orthodox position left things in the
chronic hermeneutical disarray that characterizes the Christian
canon. The disarray exists not only because the Old Testament is
interpreted in a way that is intrinsically foreign to it, but also because the entire Old Testament is left intact, inviting further open-
ended interpretation. Indeed, of all the world's religions, Christianity alone has both included the sacred writings of another tradition (Judaism), and simultaneously reinterpreted them. A kind of
bifocal vision is the result. On the one hand, the God of the Old Testament is acknowledged to be the God of the New Testament. But,
on the other, certain claims are made about the relation of the Old

Testament to Jesus that are far from evident. The Old Testament is viewed as the multifarious account of God's dealings with his people, while the New Testament is the veiled panoramic record of God's preparation for the advent of Jesus Christ. So strange and hidden was this preparation that only with the eyes of faith could one go back to the Jewish Scriptures and find this plan of God.

Motivated by the problems associated with its sacred writings, the Christian community was immediately involved in hermeneutics. In one sense, every passage was viewed as authoritative. Yet the plan that God devised to prepare the way for Jesus was certainly more apparent in some Old Testament passages than in others. Ultimately, a number of these passages took on a heightened sense of importance in the canon, due to their use in the New Testament (for example, Is. 53). The basic ambiguity of these texts for the Christian faith has really never been resolved. If Christianity had been at heart a religion of its holy writings, in the manner of Islam, then it could never have tolerated these tensions. As such, however, the tensions remain as perennial problems for Christian theology to address.

Christian theology has traditionally developed out of its close biblical involvement with this chronological hermeneutics. Typology itself is grounded in this manner of interpreting human existence. Molly Wallace Boucher writes:

> Typology is the perception of God's acts in history as consistent (in biblical terms, steadfast), therefore, as interrelated and mutually illuminating; but also as each new, individual, and particular. Typology is continuous not simply because of the continuity of cause and effect in history, but because purpose is lent by history's author, God.[2]

Indeed, without a historical, contextual view, typological interpretation is not possible. Only if history has a meaningful direction

---

[2]Molly Wallace Boucher, "Metonymy in Typology and Allegory, with a Consideration of Dante's *Comedy*," in Morton W. Bloomfield, ed., *Allegory, Myth, and Symbol*, Harvard English Studies 9 (Cambridge: Harvard University Press, 1981) 129-45, esp. 133.

can the type/antitype relationship portrayed in the New Testament take meaningful direction. Boucher elaborates this point by quoting Frank Kermode's study of the Gospels and Dante's *Divine Comedy*.

> There was a need for realism (in these books), and an equal need for *testimonia*, so that this sequence of events should seem a piece or even the crown of an historical development perceptible to the eye of the interpreter and written into the structure of the world, now seen as a book, now as a codex.[3]

Kermode rightly perceives that a major intention of the Gospels, especially the Synoptics, is to establish the relevant ties between the Jesus event and Jewish historicality. We have in them throughout, purely and simply, chronology in the service of theology. Once, using Rudolf Bultmann's phrase, the "proclaimer became the proclaimed," Orthodoxy determined the theological worth of establishing the Jesus figure in time. The Gnostic wing of the church denied the historical, typological schema, and alienated faith in the pastness of Judaism. Orthodoxy constructed its chronology on two fronts: (1) the type/antitype relationship with Israel's past, and (2) the historical representation of the earthly life of Jesus found in the Gospels. In the former, the historical framework was already at hand for theological interpretation. In the latter, history became even more intimately associated with theology, with even fewer "objective" moorings. In this regard, the plurality of the Gospel witness itself is of extraordinary interest and importance. Obviously, Orthodoxy did not require that the Gospels correspond in precise historical detail. However, it did maintain the minimal requirement of the historicity of Jesus. Only upon the establishment of this perspective could the ties with Judaism that echo throughout the New Testament be developed and fostered. Gnostic theology failed this acid test. For Orthodoxy, the teachings of Jesus would maintain their validity only in the context of historicized narrative flowing out of the Old Testament.

---

[3]Cf. Frank Kermode, *The Genesis of Secrecy: On the Interpretation of Narrative* (Cambridge: Harvard University Press, 1979) 121.

Early Christian typology was not only concerned with establishing a context for understanding the identity of Jesus, it penetrated to the core of that identity itself. Etymologically, the name *Jesus* (itself a Greek transcription of the Hebrew Joshua [Yeshua]) means "Yahweh is Salvation." It is understandable that the essentially apolitical posture of the New Testament church forcefully retarded the development of the natural type/antitype relationship between the Old Testament Joshua and Jesus in Christian thought. But aside from political and military consideration, Jesus was viewed as a new type of Joshua. The Hebrew name had implied that "Yahweh was salvation" for the Hebrews alone. The Greek name Jesus, however, carried with it a forceful *universalizing* capacity. Derivatively, Yahweh was therefore viewed in salvific terms for the Gentiles as well. However, in spite of this universalizing dimension, the faith would nonetheless be grounded in the particularity of the Christ event. No Christian could doubt this: It is the beginning point for all Christian thought, no matter how divergent the various theologies would become. The question of how to *define* this particularity of Jesus remained, however. The canonical Gospels addressed the question from four distinct perspectives. Had the intention of Orthodoxy been narrowly biographical, a stricter harmony or a single compilation would have been required. But the church determined to live with the biographic tensions in much the same way that it lived in tension with the Old Testament. The fourfold nature of the Gospel response dictated that a certain variegated hermeneutical approach be tolerated, even encouraged, by Orthodoxy. Diversity would be the lifeblood that would enable the particularity of the faith to emerge in the midst of local diversity. But such a toleration was one that was held closely in check by the framework of the historicity of Jesus.

This process by which Orthodoxy dealt with the variety of traditions about Jesus that emerged in the first centuries represented a middle way. On the one hand, some Christians wished to Judaize the faith by linking it directly with the historical and cultic traditions of Israel, while others severed these ties completely by denying the historicity of Jesus. Historical typology had the characteristics of each without succumbing to perceived inadequacies. Upon its broad foundation was constructed the basis of Christian thought that has survived until our own day. This entire structure was grounded in chronology—a concept that was then taken in a richer sense than is the case in the modern West. We may describe this process as one that *enframes*. The Christian Judaizers, Gnostics, and radical apocalypticists had forced the chronological issue in independent ways. The Judaizers had integrated Christian time into traditional Judaic time. The result was a Jewish-Christian synthesis that left the faith as little more than a sect of the mother religion. The Gnostics had shattered traditional Judaic time and established a separate, atemporal reality. The result was theological isolation from major intellectual resources of the Roman world. The radical apocalypticists had reduced the Judaic tradition to a science of signs for the coming of the end. The result was a Qumranlike phenomenon that died the death of its own failed projections. In this environment, Orthodoxy sought a way of accommodation— one might almost say, a way of convenience—among an extraordinary spectrum of forces and counterforces. The proclamation of Jesus, which had generated the entire effort, could not stand uninterpreted. As a result, historical typology encapsulated the response to the experiences of Jesus and established the means by which the faith would posture itself in the mainstream of Judaic time. This typology served the primary function of legitimation and allowed the developing church to utilize established Judaism without identifying with it. It placed Judaic history at its disposal and neutralized the naturally superior posture of a parent religious tradition. Through this means Christianity claimed Judaic history *as its own*. Depending upon one's perspective, it either captured or liberated the purpose of this history. This history established the identity of the church in the world by locating it in the chronology of Judaism.

The orthodox hermeneutic transformed the response to Jesus into a rational, chronological structure: (1) ancient Israel/Old Testament, (2) John the Baptist, (3) the life of Jesus, and (4) the era of the church. This chronology provided more than the background for Jesus' teachings; it itself became a hermeneutics of them by linking their content to the imposed chronological system. The elements of this system are clearly visible in the *narrated* (not necessarily "authentic") words of Jesus. For example, the so-called antitheses of Matt. 5:21-48 point to a clear demarcation between the past and the present ("You have heard that it was said. . . . But I say to you . . ."). Similarly, Luke 11:29b-30 (plus parallels) establishes a strict separation between the future and the present ("This generation is an evil generation; it seeks a sign, but no sign shall be given to it except the sign of Jonah"). These sayings were utilized in a particular way by Orthodoxy. With the historical typology of the Gospels in mind, it is instructive to inquire into the question of time in the teachings of Jesus, drawing heavily on those who have sought the authentic words of Jesus that lie embedded in the Gospels of the church.

Jesus' hermeneutics of time. New Testament scholarship has conclusively demonstrated that the center of Jesus' proclamation concerned the Kingdom of God. Ongoing research into the meaning of this message continues to enrich our understanding of its impact on the religious environment of Jesus' day. Recent discoveries of Coptic texts at Nag Hammadi have shown us additional, extracanonical ways in which the message was interpreted in early Christianity. However, nearer at hand, the New Testament itself exhibits a variety of hermeneutical approaches to its meaning. This entire phenomenon is to be seen within the context of the overall nature of its *response* to Jesus and his proclamation. The centrality of the salvific crucifixion motif in Paul's theology is an example of this response, just as is the "Son of Man" Christology of Mark. Analogous ways of responding to Jesus could be (and have been) amplified throughout the traditions of the New Testament. The result of all this is the indisputable view that the New Testament is throughout already highly theological, constructed out of the hermeneutical activity of the early church.

We may take Mark 1:15 as the essential formulation of Jesus' proclamation: "The time is fulfilled and the kingdom of God is at hand; repent, and believe in the gospel." This message consists of three major parts: (1)the fulfillment of time; (2) the presence of the kingdom; and (3) the called-for response of repentance. Each of these components is programmatic in its own right in determining the general boundaries of Jesus' message. However, the components do not carry equal weight. The first of them is constitutive for the remaining two. This can be clearly seen if we alter the terminology in terms of the underlying ground of meaning: (1) the activity of time (fulfillment); (2) the activity of God (presence in the world); (3) the activity of man (repentance/belief). This way of viewing the message uncovers its inherent dynamic. Jesus views the world in terms of *activity*—that is, in terms of movement, change, transformation, and the like. Obviously, the focus of the message is on this world. But of equal importance is the chronological *immediacy* peculiar to his message. In fact, on consideration of additional teachings that have a high likelihood of authenticity, we see that Jesus is incorporating the past, present, and future from the standpoint of this immediacy of God. Returning to the dynamic structure of Mark 1:15, we see concealed its temporal dimension: (1) the *past* has opened to the present (fulfillment of time); (2) the *future* has opened to the present (reign of God); and (3) the *present* presents itself as immediacy (repent and believe). These three elements constitute the temporal dimension of Jesus' message, but they also show that Jesus' message is grounded in temporality itself.

The distinctive approach of Jesus to time, an approach that transcends linear chronology, goes to the heart of his teaching. Twentieth-century time is set in the context of the utilitarian *management* of time. We measure time according to modules of convenience (years, months, days, hours, and so on). Of course, it is common in Christian thought to develop theologically a concept of "meaningful" time (Καιρός) that is not limited to the simply chronological. We still hear the echoes of this perspective in the English adjective "historic"—that is, a time with peculiar significance for later time. However, the fundamental message of Jesus carries yet a third way of understanding time, one that transcends both the historical and the historic, even as it incorporates both. Jesus pointed to the raw immediacy of time itself. He defined time in such a way that past, present, and future are all contained in this immediacy. This is a revolutionary concept that *unifies* an otherwise disjunctive view of time (whether chronological or existential). For him, reality is immediate. When he speaks of the future, he does so from the standpoint of its immediacy: "The kingdom of God is at hand." When he speaks of the past, it is the same: "The time is fulfilled," the past is immediate. His teaching is fundamentally a hermeneutics of time.

In this way, Jesus reestablishes the wholeness and essential unity of time that had been sundered by the religious thought of his day. For him, time is a continuum, of which past, present, and future are simply distinguishable aspects that remain open to one another. This view of time may be visualized as a body. The one hand is the past; the other is the future. The head is the present. The presence of the body itself represents the immediacy of time. What we term the future is, in reality, a way of defining the immediate *posture* of the entire body in the direction of the future hand. This posture is reshaping the grip of the past, and the involvement of the present. The future hand, according to Jesus, ought to be in a perpetual attitude of openness, that is, repentance and belief. These terms represent ways of posturing oneself toward the future in a receptive way. They characterize this posture as a molding of the self around the contours of an open future. Because the future is necessarily uncertain, one must decide to live in a perpetual state of activity that continually affirms one's trust in the future. The natural human temptation is to take refuge in one or another of the aspects of time, in such a way that the unity that exists in its immediacy is fractured. Natural human behavior is predicated on the avoidance of immediacy. Jesus addressed these concerns in the Lord's Prayer, parables, and Kingdom sayings. These are precisely the texts to which New Testament scholarship grants the greatest likelihood of authenticity.[4]

The Lord's Prayer found in Luke 11:2b-4 (with greater likelihood of authenticity than Matthew 6) confirms the temporal structure of Jesus' teaching. We may chronologically divide the prayer in this way:

A Supplication to God

I. Invocation	2b
II. Main Body	2c-4b
A. Supplication proper	2c-4a
1. That the Future-Present be Immediate	2c

---

[4]I am following Norman Perrin's basic criteria for isolating the likely authentic sayings of Jesus. Cf. Perrin, *Rediscovering the Teaching of Jesus* (New York: Harper & Row, 1967) 15-49, esp. 47.

This structure illustrates the way in which Jesus overcomes the strictly quantitative meaning of time, and metaphorically reveals its deeper qualitative reality. The limitation of quantity is that it divides and separates, whereas the qualitative metaphor uncovers an underlying unity. We see that Jesus portrays the future-present (aorist imperative) in terms of God's name and reign. The trust of man in the future-present of God explicitly results in day-by-day (τὸ καθ᾽ ἡμέραν) bodily subjection ("give us bread"). The present-progressive sense of δίδου steps from the past, to the present, to the future. For Jesus, this is the *human meaning* of chronological existence. The prayer requests that this entire chronological sweep be made immediate. It is important to see that it is only the present-future that receives a two-part emphasis. It is the major thrust of the prayer. God is spirit and transcends the convenient human interpretive distinctions of past, present, future. However, within those categories of time, human beings experience God in the immediacy of the future becoming present. Man, who is body, postures himself in trustful receptivity to the immediately future-present God. This is the theological meaning of the finite body that is continually subjected to the movement of time. The body *compels* us to choose either for or against the (God's) future. Because of the body, even to avoid choosing is to choose. In such instances, death makes our choice for us.

Similarly, the past becoming present is understood qualitatively by Jesus. The human past is characterized by sin (ἁμαρτία). Sin is the important thing that we bring into the present from the past. I might say that sin is both past and present. Jesus does not say that every action which we have committed is sinful. Rather, he maintains that certain activities of the past block or hinder it from being *resolved* in the present, namely, those which are designated sinful. Sin, in other words, has the capacity of *making* the past an idol by allowing it too much emphasis in the present. In such instances, one's present behavior is *determined* by the past. To reverse this very principle, a past that is liberation from sin results in an open potential for the immediate experience of God. Of course, one must be free *for* this immediacy by escaping, as well, the idolatry of the present. Jesus speaks of the present existentially in terms of others being indebted to us—as a motivation for the entire prayer. Again, this type of indebtedness makes an idol of time. As long as others remain indebted to us, we remain removed from immediacy. Indebtedness becomes just as vigorous an opponent of immediacy as our past sins. Of course, indebtedness is a term grounded in law; from indebtedness springs *legal* domination and exploitation. Jesus' teaching at this point implies the ultimate transcendence of law as the way in which we experience the present. Paradoxically, the very *fairness* of the law itself becomes a stumbling block to immediacy because it keeps one entrapped in established patterns of social behavior and relationships, thereby isolating both the past and the future from the present. It is precisely those patterns that Jesus wishes to overturn.

The richness of immediacy. The Kingdom of God is Jesus' metaphorical name for the claims of the immediate activity of God. This perspective becomes evident in those sayings and parables of Jesus that have the strongest case for authenticity. Norman Perrin, in *The Kingdom of God in the Teachings of Jesus,* has isolated three Kingdom sayings as "undisputably authentic": Luke 17:20-21/11:20 and Matthew 11:12. The first of these integrates the future into the present: "The Kingdom of God is not coming with signs to be observed; nor will they say, 'Lo, here it is!' or 'There!' for behold, the kingdom of God is *in the midst of you.*" Such a statement is not merely informational: it demands an existential response. Such a perspective represents a dramatic transformation of Judaic eschatological thought. Luke 11:20 is hardly less dramatic: "But if it is by the finger of God that I cast out demons, then the kingdom of God has come upon you." It is clear that Jesus placed exorcism and healing at the service of his proclamation of the Kingdom. In this passage his practice of exorcism is not viewed as an end in itself, but as a way to break free of the chronological framework of past causes and present effect. Past, present, and future become unified in the immediate experience of God. Finally, Matthew 11:12 is an explicit analysis of the apocalyptic movements of the day symbolized by that of John the Baptist: "From the days of John the Baptist until now the kingdom of heaven has suffered violence (βιάζεται); and men of violence take it by force (ἁρπάζουσιν)." "Force" employed against the Kingdom is what subjects it to the chronological distortion of disjunctive time. This distortion is, of course, purely rational. It is the unsuccessful attempt to avoid the immediacy of God in the hiddenness of time. Apocalypticism accomplishes this with reference to the future. Thus we see that these authentic sayings of Jesus establish the identity of immediacy by negatively differentiating it from chronological perversions.

In his sayings and axioms, Jesus also aggressively attacks the chronological structure of rational, chronological causality. What we conventionally term ethics flows out of the violence of this attack. Examples of such sayings are still evident in the Synoptics; for example:

Leave the dead to bury their own dead (Luke 9:60a).

No one who puts his hand to the plow and looks back is fit for the kingdom of God (Luke 9:62).

Whoever does not receive the kingdom of God like a child shall not enter it (Mark 10:15).

Do not resist one who is evil. But if any one strikes you on the right cheek, turn to him the other also; and if any one would sue you and take your coat, let him have your cloak as well; and if one forces you to go one mile, go with him two miles (Matt. 5:39b-41).

It is easier for a camel to go through the eye of a needle than for a rich man to enter the Kingdom of God (Mark 10:25).

Such sayings destroy conventional ethics in that they penetrate to the internal thought processes that determine behavior. We know, of course, as Pirsig indicates, that thinking is a form of action. A direct corollary of the manner in which Jesus reintegrated time in his proclamation of immediacy was the holistic way he spoke of thought and behavior. All of the sayings picture some sort of behavior; but that behavior is so strikingly antithetical to convention that we are challenged to consider the thought that resides within the behavior. The response to these sayings is not simply to behave, but rather to raise such questions as: How can this be? How can one not bury the dead? How can one become a child again? How can the rich give up their wealth? One searches for ways to mollify such statements, but not because the behavior is difficult in and of itself. Rather one seeks to avoid the direct claims of immediacy that such behavior represents. For Jesus, ethics is derived from time. Unethical behavior allows us to avoid immediacy in the refuge of past/present/future existence. All of the authentic sayings of Jesus have this meaning at the core. It is the intention of these sayings to eliminate this refuge. They destroy the cloaking ability of time, especially the legal character of present time (cf. the discussion of the Lord's Prayer). Like legal forms, sayings are eternally *present*. Sayings have universal application; they are valid in all places and times. But Jesus' sayings are more; they break through the present into the experience of immediacy.

Similarly, the underlying intention of the parables of Jesus is to illustrate those aspects of human existence that obscure the Kingdom or the immediate encounter with God. In so doing, he indicates that the ways we invent to avoid it are innumerable. It is in this restricted sense that he speaks of human evil and sin. It is not that the world itself is evil. Indeed, the world viewed as a language event offered itself as an extraordinary treasury of metaphors of the Kingdom, as in the seed images of Mark 4:3-8, 26-29, and 30-32. These parabolic images swallow up conventional chronology in the miraculous. Each seed that grows is a miracle, and if we do not see it as such, then it is because our contemporary technological culture has taught us to *expect* the growth. Jesus says: "The kingdom of God is as if a man should scatter seed on the ground, and should sleep and rise night and day; and the seed should sprout and grow, he knows not how" (Mark 4:26b-27). The miraculous character of this event precisely resides in this "he knows not how," in that aspect of the everyday event that resides beyond the capacity of analytic reasoning. For Jesus, a miracle does not mean suspension of the normal flow of events contrary to natural processes. It means the ground of everyday that remains free from conventional chronology. The miraculous transformation of the small seed of the mustard shrub to the greatness of the plant echoes the same perspective (Mark 4:30-32). The same point is developed in the Parable of the Sower (Mark 4:3-8). Here the emphasis is not on the process of growth itself; rather it is on the quality of the soil that nurtures (or fails to nurture) the seed. Only if the seed falls into "good" soil does the seed yield grain, *no matter* how much time is granted. Again the chronological plays no formative role in the meaning of the parable; it is subsumed into the qualitative ("good" soil). We might say that only good soil prepares the ground for the miracle of growth (" . . . increasing and yielding thirtyfold and sixtyfold and hundredfold," 4:8b). In this way, we see that it is not that the Kingdom results from a disjunctive miracle that comes by way of God breaking through solely in the present, but that miracles happen wherever the Kingdom is. Goodness in this sense means the free, unhindered acceptance of the Kingdom, the immediacy of God. The natural phenomena of birds, rocky soil, and the sun symbolize in their relationship to the seed the effect of evil in the world. Obviously, these things are not inherently evil; but the effect that they have upon seeds presents a metaphor for Jesus' teaching. He is not concerned with evil as such, but only with those things that stifle and destroy immediacy. In this way, Jesus radically transforms the meaning of evil, subjecting it to his overall hermeneutics of time.

The chronological fluidity of the parables also affords an illustration of the way that Jesus portrays the three dimensions of time enfolding upon themselves in immediacy. They are most often grounded in the narrative past: "There was a man"/"Two men went up into the temple to pray"/"A man planted a vineyard." The parables can also be constructed out of the hypothetical present or future: "The kingdom of God is as if a man should scatter seed"/"But to what shall I compare this generation? It is like children sitting in the market places and calling to their playmates"/"Which of you has a friend will go to him at midnight?" No matter the chronological setting, the parables cause us to experience the fullness of time in terms of immediacy. In this way, like the sayings, many of them explicitly shatter the structure of conventional chronology. Here past, present, and future open to one another. An excellent example of the chronological fluidity of a single parable is that of the Laborers in the Vineyard (Matt. 20:1-16).

1. Narrative *past*—A story that *happened* (fictionally or non-fictionally) in the past.
2. Depicted *present*—The events of the story are present to its characters, and are designed to relate to the present experience of the hearer/reader.
3. Projected *future*—The explicit point of the story: "So the last *will be* first, and the first last."

The thrust of the parable is the legal dilemma of the present. Although located in the past, the story narrates the mechanics of everyday existence—daily wage earners in a vineyard. All who heard it would have been aware of the dynamics of the story from their own daily lives. The parable is based on the premise that legal, contractual wage agreements are constructed according to quantified chronology. One earns a set amount of money for a set amount of time on the job. This is the conventional, rational way that people do business. It is this quantified chronology that the householder of the parable upsets when he pays all the laborers the same, regardless of their period of work. It is the same kind of chronology that Jesus transcends throughout his teachings about immediacy. Here, for example, fairness is transcended by generosity. Fairness is bound by the rules of conventional chronology. Generosity, on the other hand, knows no such rules. It is completely open-ended. The householder could choose to pay a year's salary for one hour's work. The point would be the same. For Jesus, authentic time cannot be measured.

The same view of time undergirds, with greater or lesser visibility, other parables of Jesus. Examples include: The Unmerciful Servant (Matt. 18:23-35), The Prodigal Son (Luke 15:11-32), The Unjust Steward (Luke 16:1-13), The Marriage Feast (Luke 22:1-14), The Friend at Midnight (Luke 11:5-8), and The Leaven (Luke 11:20b-21). It is not the case that the explicit intention of such parables is to teach a new way of perceiving time. Jesus is not a metaphysician of time. But it is evident that he wished to uncover the experience of immediacy, and that this only happens in the usually ignored unity of time. In his parables, Jesus addressed common ways in which we maintain the conventional chronological order. Even a parable as

seemingly far removed from such considerations as The Good Samaritan (Luke 10:29-37) ultimately, after peeling back to its deepest
layers, overcomes present complicity and discloses a new temporal
unity. This unity has conceptual ties with the teaching on generosity found in the Laborers of the Vineyard. The meaning of temporal unity in this case is intensified by reference to the widespread
disregard of the Samaritans by the Jews. But the exemplary actions
of the Samaritan transcend the boundaries of disjunctive time. Jesus continually pointed to such actions in his parables and throughout his teachings.

• Toward a New Theology of American Time •

My analysis of Pirsig's *Zen and the Art of Motorcycle Maintenance*
stresses the centrality of the category of time for his assessment of
contemporary American experience. Although his novelistic form
has autobiographical features, its major figure (Phaedrus/persona
of the author) represents yet another contribution to the substantial
body of American literary figures solidly grounded in the indige-
nous mythos. Who but an American would try to "outflank" the
entirety of Western philosophy at the University of Chicago *as a
graduate student*? Who but an American would offer his detailed discussions of Kant and Plato in the old form of the popular chautauquas of a bygone era? The book, written after a nervous breakdown
and the application of electric shock treatments, retains the resolute
air of optimism that characterizes American people.

It is clear that the protagonist is but a recent version of the traditional American mythos. Whereas the traditional mythos had interpreted that figure in biblical/typological terms, Pirsig's
contemporary figure is in "typological relationship" only *with himself*. Indeed, Pirsig's work takes on a special character because of its
very independence from the traditional ties to the Bible that denote
such earlier works as Melville's *Moby-Dick*. The persona of Pirsig's
autobiographical novel stands in historical relationship with Phaedrus: This means the Phaedrus of his pretreatment self, and only
secondarily the Phaedrus of Plato's dialogues. This artistic way of
establishing relationships to the past enables Pirsig to lay bare the
interior of the American mythos in a way unknown to previous
generations of writers who retained, explicitly or implicitly, the

connection between their representative figures and biblical types. This exposure of the mythos in Pirsig's text affords us a particular access to a reading of the Bible from a self-reflective American perspective.

The convergence between Pirsig's critique of time and Jesus' hermeneutics of time occurs precisely with the issue of disjunctive chronology. The perspective of each represents a fundamental challenge to the natural way time is viewed in Western civilization. Pirsig traces the shallowness of this prevailing view in American technological culture back to its historical roots in ancient Greece and the opposition that arose against the impermanence of the Sophists. He views the American as heir of those ancient classicists (especially Plato and Aristotle) who had attempted to defeat change by rationally encapsulating the present. They had not understood the unity of time that exists in what Pirsig terms "Quality." Modern technological culture, with its disregard for beauty and art, is the natural result. In this way, he understands our bland utility to be anchored in a distortion of mind, severed from the validity of living the "here and now."

With remarkably similar concerns, Jesus also addressed the problematic of time, only in a thoroughly religious context. He understood disjunctive time to be antithetical to the immediate experience of God (especially as it was becoming manifest in the twin traditions of legalistic and apocalyptic Judaism). For him, Pharisees were dominated by the past and traditional. As a result, the present and future were oppressed by this past and played an abbreviated role in the Pharisaic view of life. They viewed all human thought and behavior in terms of the law that had already been established. Present activity was rigorously assessed by the past. On the other side of the spectrum, the apocalypticists had reduced the religious quest to the category of God's future intervention in the affairs of the world. For them, both the past and the present were relinquished to this future. We might say that the "quality" of one's life was determined by the future and the promises or warnings about how one would participate in God's apocalyptic movement. Both the past and the present were reduced to the problematic of *sign* (for the future).

Into this environment Jesus came preaching that the Kingdom of God was at hand. This meant that the future was unfolding and already a part of the present (and the past) in the immediate encounter with God. When one encounters God in this way, then the present takes on a qualitatively new dimension. Similarly, this encounter reveals the activity of God in one's past that had heretofore existed only in secret. This message of Jesus was a direct affront to the historical schemata of the apocalypticists, just as it was to the legal traditions of the Pharisees. Much as Pirsig views the ancient Greek anti-Sophists, Jesus had seen the Pharisees and apocalypticists encapsulating the meaning of time. From the standpoint of each interpreter, the opposing views had failed to perceive the unity of time and had disjoined it. Each responds by attempting to restore the meaning of the immediacy of experience.

While Pirsig's and Jesus' conceptions of time have common features, major distinctions obviously remain to be made. Such distinctions penetrate deeper than the simplistic secular/sacred opposition. The key to the differences in the approaches of Pirsig and Jesus lies in the contrast of the intellectual environments in which each challenged the prevailing conception of time. We may summarize as follows: Pirsig's environment is characterized by technological time, largely uninformed by the historical past, whereas the Judaic environment of Jesus is dipolar in terms of past (legalistic) and future (apocalyptic) time. While the latter of these two environments has been extensively discussed throughout theological literature, much less has been brought to the attention of theologians concerning the former. Indeed, only the exterior movement from a contemporary text (Pirsig) to the New Testament has enabled this perspective to emerge in its true importance for us. We term this intellectual movement as *exterior* because it is larger than the intentionality of Pirsig's text itself. Nonetheless, Pirsig convincingly argues that the category of time is the irreducible reality of life that stands at the base of all our forms of cultural expression, and that the particular difficulty of American existence is the rapidity of movement from the present into the future. In his view, we are suffering from the technological distortions that result. The intellectual capital that would retard this movement out of the present toward the future simply does not exist in the American experience.

The validity of Pirsig's position may be affirmed in spite of the significant roles that both historical typology and religious millenarianism have played here. In order to understand the American mythos at its core, attention must be focused on the vacuum of its present. Historical typology ultimately proves itself to be destructive, rather than constructive, of the past. It is a technique that is the stuff of *manufactured*, not living, history and tradition. At its core, it is the encapsulating impulse typical of contemporary theology. Richard Hofstadter is surely correct when he describes the emerging twentieth-century American attitude as one that "stimulated the development of an intellectual style in which the past was too often regarded simply as a museum of confusion, corruption, and exploitation."[5] In fact, Americans have encapsulated the past with the same singleness of purpose that the New Testament writers absorbed the ancient traditions of Israel, only in this new environment it would be subject to the techniques of commercialization. Museums, for example, are commercial endeavors that serve to isolate one from the past, just as surely as they offer a window to it in packaged form.

Because the past has been isolated in this way from the American experience, the future has traditionally borne the contemporary burden of religious enthusiasm and expectation. Moreover, such enthusiasm and expectation have been primary forces in generating the American mythos from the beginning down to our own day. They are the confirming marks of God's new and mighty work in this environment with its intrinsic significance for the entire world. This grip of the future on American religious thought has been stifling. However, it has been unceasingly maintained because it has conformed so neatly with the corresponding grip of the future on mainstream technological American culture. The future has traditionally been the one temporal sphere that is uncategorically opened here to the life of the church. In America, even the an-

---

[5]Richard Hofstadter, *Anti-intellectualism in American Life* (New York: Alfred A. Knopf, 1969) 239.

titypical figures of historical typology have assumed their shape in the sense of leading the Great Experiment toward its ultimate fulfillment in God's future. This has been both the source of the vitality of American religion and its creeping irrelevance.

Considered theologically, Pirsig's text teaches us that what has failed specifically in American church history, and generally throughout Western Christendom, is an adequate response to the present. A present lacking adequate religious expression has fostered the enormous untamed growth of the technical-industrial complex in American life—a cultural expression without benefit of the checks and balances that characterize most other spheres of activity. In this situation, the easy attractiveness of thought directed to "God's future" early became a symbol of America's theological impotence. Therefore, traditional Christian thought in this setting has been as weak precisely at that point as the broader secular society. The technological present loses itself in continually changing toward the future. In the technological view, the future is alienated from the present and related to it artificially by means of manipulation. As a result, although at one level the center of attention is upon the present, the present experience of reality is ultimately left incomplete and unsatisfying because of the overbearing mythos of *progress* and *improvement*. One lives in and for the future, a future that looms over the present as a negating threat. The future is synonymous with the power of obsolescence, the passing away of the meaning of the present. In this way, the future is problematic for the present, as well as the opportunity for its bettering. The future in this instance is not the natural future (the future unfolding into the present), but a rational construct of the future. Pirsig's text is a call to replace this distorted present/future with the genuine immediacy of the "here and now." Obviously his silence concerning Christian thought witnesses to his lack of confidence in its ability to address this fundamental problem.

We have seen that Jesus was concerned with the present in a way different from traditional (even biblical) Christianity. Far more explicitly than Pirsig, he addresses the present in its essential oneness with the past and the future. This sharply defined focus is a response to the religious environment that had distorted the present either in terms of the past (Pharisaism) or the future (apocalypticism). Like Pirsig, he points to the essential temporal artificiality of those around him. Unlike Pirsig, he far more explicitly points to the unity of time in his proclamation of the immediacy of the Kingdom of God. Whereas Pirsig's "here and now" (a concept rooted in Zen) is designed to eradicate the *imposition* of a technological future on the present, Jesus' view of the Kingdom is *receptive* to the natural unfolding of the future into the present. In this sense, the content of Jesus' teaching penetrates further than Pirsig's text. Pirsig's work is directed toward the distortions of time; Jesus, on the other hand, begins with the proclamation of authentic time itself. Hence Jesus' use of the concept of the Kingdom of God is not identical with Pirsig's "here and now." This distinction between "immediacy" (Kingdom of God) and "present" (here and now) I have maintained throughout this discussion.

Our hermeneutical reflections on the exterior encounter of Pirsig's *Zen and the Art of Motorcycle Maintenance* with the presumed authentic teachings of Jesus have enabled us to fix the chronological locus of the American mythos and its ultimate unfolding in the modern technological society. This mythos is revealed as a way of establishing the dominance of the technological future at the expense of both the past and the present. This technological future ignores those aspects of the past that defy the culturally established patterns of the type-antitype relationship. Similarly, the natural consequences of present activity in the future are downplayed in the benign comfort of God's ultimate affirmation of the mythos itself. As such, the religious imagination in America is stymied by the disjunctive chronology of early, biblical theologians. This chronology, together with the utopian demands of the American mythos, functions to replace what Jesus termed the Kingdom of God with a sacrally supported kingdom of man.

· CONCLUSION ·

It is the task of Christian theology to give a meaningful response to the vital issues of each succeeding generation in light of its faith experience. In this book I have attempted to think theologically by engaging primary American literary texts with fundamental selections from the Bible. I know of no better way to fulfill the hermeneutical character of Christian thought. As it was the vision of St. Thomas to posit the newly discovered texts of Aristotle as the raw material upon which to engage the faith, then certainly we should not shy from the same sort of activity with texts that capture the revolution in human thought that is the American mythos. Indeed, contemporary biblical scholarship has provided us with extensive evidence of the same sort of hermeneutical activity between faith and culture *within* the Bible itself. One of the undisputed fruits of the historical-critical method is its demonstration of the way that the writers of the Bible utilized the language and thought patterns of their surrounding cultures in their own texts. Clearly they did not simply declare yes *or* no to the plurality of theologies and religious institutions in their environments; rather they declared yes *and* no. They were both critical and selective in their relation to the extrinsic literary environment. These early theologians were culturally aware in a very broad sense. We, as readers of the Bible, should also take our culture critically into account in our theological work. To follow through on this prescription, we must carefully consider the American interpretive context that is always present when we read the Bible.

This journey into American biblical hermeneutics has raised an old theological problem with renewed force and acuteness for our time and place. Throughout the discussion of all our texts—American, as well as biblical—the problem of the universality of the Christian faith has stood in the background; sometimes hidden beneath the surface, at other times quite visible. This problem generated the churchless-Jesus theologies of the mythic religious consciousness of Jefferson and Franklin in early America. It is present in the protests against the distortion of the mythos in Melville and Pirsig. It is explicitly addressed in the biblical texts of Job and a number of the likely authentic texts of the historical Jesus. I maintain, therefore, that *the* theological problem, above all others in our culture, is how to conceive of the Christian faith in a genuinely universal manner. While I cannot pretend to have exhausted this subject in this small book, I do claim to have fully documented its central importance for our theological considerations. I hope that I have offered some worthwhile projections as to how we might conceive of a truly universal Christian faith.

In considering the biblical foundations of this issue, it is instructive to note that the problem of particularity and universalism was one that was eventually faced within the Hebrew Scriptures themselves. The Book of Job is a major literary source in this regard. I hope that my discussion of it has helped establish some basic categories. We need, for example, a theological analysis of the concept of "chosenness," including a more complete discussion of the idea of Israel as a "light to the nations." This light obviously was intended to be the illumination of what it means to live with God, not simply the refraction of Israel's human culture. The universalism of Jonah, Ecclesiastes, and Isaiah also come immediately to mind. Christian discourse built upon such universal concepts in the Hebrew writings from the beginning (note, for example, the prologue of the Gospel of John and the genealogy of Jesus in Luke 3). We should do more to integrate fully these texts into the mainstream of our religious thought. Certainly American biblical hermeneutics means that we should read the biblical texts themselves in a new

way, and not simply be content with reading the texts of our particular culture.

It has also become clear to me that Melville's "Old Testament
novel" should be taken in a programmatic sense for American theology. The journey to a genuinely universal Christian theology goes
through the Old Testament. We must fully appropriate these texts;
we must, indeed, speak in terms of a liberation of the Old Testament. A major intention of the writings generated by the early
church itself—some of which found their way into a second collection of canonical writings (the "New" Testament)—was to serve
heuristically for a more universal reading of these ancient Scriptures. As such, in the broad stream of Christian orthodoxy, the
"New" Testament was not intended to summarize or displace the
contents of the "Old" Testament, but to broaden them into the matrix of the Gentile church. That the church did not omit the Old Testament from its complete canon confirms a confidence in its ability
to achieve this. Yet it would be a mistake to minimize the radical effect that the development of additional canonical writings had on
the Old Testament. In the dialectic of old and new, the new obviously played a preponderant role. After all, it *did* provide the
frame through which the old was interpreted—fundamentally by
the innate authority resulting from its explicit reference and response to Jesus. Jesus could only be found in the Old Testament
through the eyes of faith. And Jesus, of course, was one particular
human being with a particular history in a specific cultural context.
Once Christian orthodoxy became centered in the man rather than
in the message, the faith became inextricably embedded in the
problem of universality and particularity. Both Jefferson and Franklin showed remarkable sensitivity to this fact in their theological
judgments. The canonical writings of the early church, however,
would aid the believer in this not so very evident task of finding the
man, not the teachings, in the Old Testament. The early church's
need to develop the New Testament canon is itself a witness to the
difficulties inherent in the approach.

The terms *old* and *new* demonstrate the dynamic in orthodoxy's
universalizing hermeneutics of the Old Testament. The question of
time is not only central to science, but to theology as well. At a profound level in the early church, the fundamental question of ortho-

doxy hinged on a particular interpretation of time. Revelation itself, both in the written form of Scripture and the eternal Word of the Incarnation, was woven into the fabric of time by these early theologians. The programmatic superiority that the new writings of the early church held over the old writings of Israel rested ultimately on chronological grounds. Jesus was not king, priest, and prophet from the time of his appearance onward; he was the formative figure in each of these categories vis-à-vis all those who had come *before* him as well. The appearance of Jesus of Nazareth in human history fulfilled the goals and aspirations of the Old Testament tradition. Orthodoxy interpreted the Old Testament as *unfolding* into the Christ event; all pre-Christian time was interpreted as *preparation* for the expected one. As we know, this chronological scheme had a certain incompletion, awaiting the full consummation of the Kingdom of God at a yet undetermined point in the future. Orthodoxy hermeneutically captured time by *dividing* it into three totally separate parts: Preparation (past), Christ-event (midpoint), and apocalyptic expectation (future). In this scheme the so-called present functions as a sort of passageway between the midpoint of the Christ-event and the full consummation of the age and has a certain *provisional* character. This "provisional nature" of the present helps explain the hesitancy of the church fathers to embrace fully Greco-Roman science and technology, and the subsequent slow emergence of scientific inquiry from the "preparation" of the Middle Ages.

This division of time by Christian orthodoxy represents a rational theological construct that defines the earliest theological response to the life and teaching of Jesus—a hermeneutical strategy that is especially distorted in the unfolding of the mythos of exceptionality and mission. Its division into points along a chronological line (past, midpoint, present, future) is quasimathematical in its level of abstraction. In fact, it is perhaps not too strong to say that it represents a kind of *mathematization* of Old Testament traditions; that is, in the sense that the chronological schemata of orthodoxy stands in analogous relationship to the plurality of Old Testament data, as mathematics stands in relationship to the data of nature. The effect of both is to conceive of the object in terms of its utility, thereby overcoming to a large extent its hold over us. It is, in other words, a somewhat aggressive form of hermeneutical encounter that has a radical effect: its intention is not merely the *understanding* of the object, but the *transformation* of it into utilitarian categories.

It would be a serious mistake to visualize the makers of early Christian thought diligently *searching* the Scriptures in order to come to some consensus about the meaning of Jesus. It must be much closer to historical accuracy to conceive of them as *confronting* those writings as a threat to the emerging church. After all, most saw in the Old Testament absolutely no compelling reason to accord Jesus any significant uniqueness, let alone assign him the midpoint of history! This very situation necessitated the application of a hermeneutical approach that was highly *abstract* in its fundamental conception—an abstraction that acted as a buffer against those outside the pale of orthodoxy.

Logically, those writings that accompanied this *new* event played the lead role in the dialectic with the past. Within the Old Testament itself, the record of God's dealings with the world greatly exceeded the narrow christological chronology of the New Testament. Here, a plurality of perspectives on time are to be found, established in both the *cyclical* time of nature and the *progressive* acts of creation found in Genesis 1. Certainly, the cyclical time of nature is irrelevant for the christological chronology envisioned by the New Testament writers. It does little to support the once-and-for-allness of the Christ-event, of which Christian orthodoxy was convicted. In addition, the general casting of the Old Testament as a record of *preparation* for this unique event tends to be undermined in proportion to emphasis placed on cyclical time. As a result, we might conclude that the hermeneutical task of the early church, in the context of its formation through the tutelage of another religion's Scriptures, forced it theologically into the problem of the interpretation of time. In many ways, the ensuing struggle with the meaning of time consumed its energies through the initial stages of its development, manifested most visibly in the struggle with Gnosticism. It is ironic that this analysis of biblical texts in hermeneutical relationship with the scientific, technological American culture of modernity shows clearly that this problem is far from resolved.

My discussion of American biblical hermeneutics reveals that Christian theology needs radical surgery in order to penetrate the metaphysical structure of the American experience. Not only is the one-dimensional hermeneutics of time found in the New Testament inadequate for authentic universality, so too is the simplistic scheme of sin/repentance/forgiveness that tends to characterize institutional religion. Until this surgery is performed with all the courage that we can muster, Christianity will remain merely an isolated appendage to the inner meaning of our cultural existence. Quite likely, the more extreme this isolation, the more vocal will be our preachers as they make up in volume and quantity what is lacking in subtlety and quality. Moreover, there is no reason to doubt that the support of such people will remain high, because Americans remain a religious people, grounded in the inherent religiosity of the American mythos. Americans demand religion, even if it is bad religion. In such an environment, theologians have an especially important task to perform—a task that this book begins, but hardly completes.

Every text has a context and a history. However disparate they may appear, all of the texts I have examined in this book—Franklin's *Autobiography*, Jefferson's *Life and Morals of Jesus*, Melville's *Moby-Dick*, the Book of Job, Pirsig's *Zen and the Art of Motorcycle Maintenance*, Jesus in the Synoptic Gospels—challenge the received religious tradition of their time and place. Each of these texts strives to interpret anew a religious tradition ultimately based on the Bible, and each of these texts makes the Bible a living testament that may once again speak to the problems and aspirations of a new generation. Each of these texts is, therefore, a biblical hermeneutics. Each represents a quest for truth in a particular time and a particular place, and yet each text reaches beyond its particulars to confront every reader with a demand for decision: how will *you* interpret this text?

No one of these interpreters says all that can be said about his work. Whenever one claims to have said the last word, "all there is to say" about a text, the result is no longer hermeneutics but dogma. As an American trained in biblical exegesis, I have attempted in this "hermeneutic of hermeneutics" to distinguish some basic features of an American biblical hermeneutics. To whatever extent I have succeeded, there is always something more to be done. In this continuing task I recall again the words of Herman Melville, as he attempted in *Moby-Dick* to set down a classification of whales. "I promise nothing complete," he wrote, "because any human thing supposed to be complete, must for that very reason infallibly be faulty." This was no attempt to excuse ignorance, or indolence, or faulty research. It was no "cop out"; it was, rather, a recognition of the depth and profundity of "a ponderous task." Melville left his "cetological System" unfinished "even as the great Cathedral of Cologne was left, with the crane still standing upon the top of the uncompleted tower." That tower stands today unfinished, even as it stood for centuries before Melville wrote. "For small erections may be finished by their first architects," Melville concluded; "grand ones, true ones, ever leave the copestone to posterity. God keep me from ever completing anything" (195-96).

This incompleteness is an invitation. Biblical hermeneutics in America remains an ongoing enterprise, ever fresh, ever renewed, ever stimulated by new experiences, new texts, new readings, new hopes. If this text, my uncompleted tower, has by its dialectical hermeneutic of hermeneutics engaged its readers in new conversations with the Bible, that will be a grace sufficient for me. In those conversations, new dialectics will emerge; America may once again live in the religious imagination and the religious imagination may once again live in America. Or so we may hope.

· SUBJECT INDEX ·

• NAME INDEX •